Thomas Cook

TRAVELLERS

BRAZIL

By
JAN [redacted] CINTYRE

Written by Jane Egginton a

Original photography by J

Editing and page layout by
Unit 2, Burr Elm Court, Ca
Series Editor: Karen Beaul

Published by Thomas Cook
A division of Thomas Cook
Company Registration No.

PO Box 227, The Thomas C
Coningsby Road, Peterboro
E-mail: books@thomascool
www.thomascookpublishing.com
Tel: +44 (0)1733 416477

ISBN: 978-1-084157-684-8

Project Editor: Linda Bass
Production/DTP Editor: Steven Collins

Printed and bound in Italy by: Printer Trento.

Front cover credits, L–R: © Theo Allofs/Getty Images; © World Pictures/Photoshot; © Gräfenhain Günter/Simephoto-4Corners Images
Back cover credits, L–R: © Damm Fridmar/Simephoto-4Corners Images; © World Pictures/Photoshot

Contents

Introduction

Brazil is an extraordinary country, not least in size. It covers more than half of South America and has one of the most diverse populations in the world, and an extraordinary mix of cultures that shines through its music and dance. This is a country that resonates deeply with people who have never even been here and leaves a deep and lasting impression on those who have. During carnaval *and the World Cup, it is a stony soul that can sit unmoved as Brazil's infectious enthusiasm is projected on television screens around the world.*

Brazilians come from a complex ethnic background made up of Indians, Portuguese and Africans, with Japanese and Germans coming into the mix. This melting pot has informed the egalitarian values and sociable spirit of most Brazilians, who cultivate solidarity and tolerance, but most of all joy.

Beaches are to Brazilians what pubs are to the British; cultural meeting points, crèches, pensioners' social clubs and even offices. Many political theorists believe it is only the readily accessible beaches that prevent the country's social problems from exploding into anarchy. Even though the vast majority of people live on the coast, in a country this size there are still secret beaches and deserted islands to be found.

Street life in Brazil is as good as it gets. Here, as on the beach, the country is equal, and people of all races and persuasions come together to eat, drink and be musical. Stalls hawking exotic local food and traditional crafts are just part of the outdoor flavour. Life on the streets finds its freest expression in the country's poorest pockets, where 'slum' dwellers are the creators of carnival. *Favela* (shanty town) life is the underlying, electrifying current of the country, and a unique urban phenomenon. To wander the cobbled streets of the country's colonial towns is by turns fascinating and stunning – they are open-air museums where history resonates.

For all its exoticism, Brazil is decidedly sophisticated, but just a little inland is another world of mountain retreats and national parks. Away from Paraty's spectacular coast are historic farms, crystal-clear waterfalls and the legendary gold trail. Into the hills from Rio is the imperial city of Petropolis while the city of Salvador leads to the Recôncavo, one of the cradles of Brazil. In the northeast, spectacular beaches quickly give way to the evocative *sertão* (backlands), while the sci-fi capital of Brasilia deep in the interior is somewhere else altogether.

Hedonism is never far away. In the workaholics' megalopolis that is São Paulo the über-rich flit from building to building by helicopter, and bars and clubs are open around the clock. Deep in the Amazon is an opera house to rival anything offered by Europe's grand capitals, and in Brazil even religion is a fascinating, throbbing spectacle. Throughout it all is a soundtrack of pulsating music – from Bahia's pounding African beats and the *favela*'s erotic baile funk to the smooth bar jazz where aficionados drink the ubiquitous and delicious cocktail that is the *caipirinha*.

A dune-backed beach in Brazil's northeast

The land

'This land, Lord, it seems to me, from one end to the other is all beach.... From the sea, the remote and arid interior seems very large; as far as the eye can see there is tree-covered land – land which seems to us to be very extensive.' *Pero Vaz de Caminha's letter to the king of Portugal in 1500 is a wonderful understatement. Brazil is the fifth-largest country in the world. Forming a very rough triangle of land, it borders every other South American nation except Chile and Ecuador.*

Ain't no mountain...

While the continent's highest peaks are in Peru and Argentina, Brazil does have significant highlands, and the largest wetland in the world, the Pantanal, watered by hundred of rivers and home to thousands of species of birds, reptiles and mammals. Then there is the Cerrado, covering a quarter of the country, which is not only the most biologically rich savannah in the world, but also the largest.

Coastal features

The Atlantic Ocean runs the entire length of Brazil's enormous 7,400km (4,600 miles) of coastline. The waters in the north tend to be calmer, backed by dunes and palm trees. Further south the coast becomes rocky, with craggy islands, hidden bays and even mountains like the Sugar Loaf. Only 8 per cent of the Atlantic forest that once covered the whole length of the coast remains today. Compared to the country as a whole, it was a narrow strip, but nonetheless it covered an area twice the size of France and rivalled the Amazon in biodiversity.

Amazonian dimensions

The Amazon basin covers over half of the country and includes both the largest river system and the biggest rainforest in the world. Over 1,000 rivers flow into the Amazon, carrying no less than 20 per cent of the world's oxygen and 30 per cent of its fresh water.

The fat of the land

When Brazil was 'discovered', the Portuguese enthused about land so good that every crop planted would flourish. Although its soil is no longer so fertile, Brazil is the world's largest coffee grower and its plantations provide enormous amounts of soya beans, sugar cane and tobacco to other nations. The dense rainforest that covers more than half the country yields rich rubber, palm oil and Brazil

0 500km
0 300 miles
CARACAS
GEORGETOWN
PARAMARIBO
CAYENNE
VENEZUELA
GUYANA
SURINAME
FRENCH GUIANA
BOGOTA
COLOMBIA
Boa Vista
Macapá
Belém
Amazon
Manaus
São Luís
Jericoacoara
Fortaleza
Teresina
Natal
BRAZIL
Olinda
Recife
Rio Branco
Porto Velho
Palmas
Maceió
Chapada Diamantina
Aracaju
PERU
Salvador
Cuiabá
LA PAZ
Goiânia
BRASÍLIA
Pantanal
BOLIVIA
Corumbá
SUCRE
Belo Horizonte
Campo Grande
Ouro Preto
Vitória
Pacific Ocean
PARAGUAY
São Paulo
Rio de Janeiro
Paraty
ASUNCIÓN
Curitiba
Iguaçu Falls
CHILE
ARGENTINA
Florianópolis
Porto Alegre
SANTIAGO
URUGUAY
BUENOS AIRES
MONTEVIDEO
Neuquén
Atlantic Ocean
Puerto Montt
City
Large Town
Small Town
POI
Motorway
Main Road
Minor Road
Airport
Railway
International Boundary
Comodoro Rivadavia
Falkland Islands (Islas Malvinas)
N
Río Gallegos

nut crops. Gold, diamonds, emeralds and amethysts are mined from the ground, glittering harvests that make the country one of the biggest producers of gems in the world.

Political geography

The workers who toiled the 'terra firma' are the pawns of one of the unhappiest chapters in Brazil's history. Captured indigenous peoples and African slaves endured some of the cruellest conditions ever documented. Today, the situation is not much happier; nearly half the farmland is owned by just 1 per cent of the population (*see 'Lula and the landless', pp106–7*). This is a country incredibly rich in resources, yet relentless corruption and mismanagement have ensured that little wealth filters down to ordinary people. Brazil may be one of the largest exporters of food in the world, yet a quarter of its people are starving.

The wetlands of the Pantanal

Iguaçu Falls from the air

History

1000 BC–AD 1000	Amazonian civilisations construct complex crop irrigation systems.
1500	On 22 April explorer Pedro Cabral lands in the northeast and claims Brazil as Portuguese territory.
1502	Cabral sails into Guanabara Bay in January, and, mistaking it for a river mouth, calls it Rio de Janeiro.
1550	African slaves are shipped to Brazil to work on sugar plantations.
1600–1700	Gold is discovered in the hills of Ouro Preto.
1624	Holland conquers the Brazilian capital of Salvador.
1661	Holland sells Brazil to Portugal for eight million guilders.
1711	French troops invade and occupy Rio de Janeiro.
1727	Coffee plantations spring up.
1728	The first diamonds are mined in the country and Brazil becomes the world's leading supplier until the South African finds of 1866.
1763	Salvador loses the title of capital to Rio de Janeiro.
1789	The first rebellion against Portuguese rule is launched by poet-dentist Tiradentes. He is hanged in Rio three years later, his body cut into pieces, and his head displayed in Ouro Preto.
1808–21	The Portuguese Crown relocates to Rio.
1822	Son of the Portuguese king declares independence from Portugal and crowns himself Pedro I, Emperor of Brazil.
1823	Homosexuality is decriminalised.
1873	Britain sends an agent, Henry Wickham, to Brazil to get rubber seeds which are cultivated in Kew Gardens and transplanted to Malaysia.

1888 Slavery is abolished.

1889 The monarchy is overthrown. Brazil becomes a republic ruled by coffee lords, cattle barons and the army.

1893 Antonio Conselheiro founds Canudos in Bahia, an independent community opposed to the new order. Canudos grows into a free enclave of 35,000 people. The republic spends millions in a four-year military campaign to destroy it. Thousands are killed.

1930 A revolt installs Getulio Vargas as provisional head of government.

1931 In Rio, the statue of Christ the Redeemer is unveiled on the summit of Corcovado Mountain.

1937 Vargas stages a coup and rules as a dictator with military backing.

1942 Brazil declares war on the Axis powers, and is the only South American country to send combat troops into Europe.

Henry Wickham smuggled rubber seeds to England in 1873

Cristo Redentor was a gift from the French in 1931

1951 Vargas, ousted in a military coup after World War II, is elected president, but kills himself three years later under army pressure.

1956–61 President Juscelino Kubitschek builds the new capital of Brasilia and presides over rapid economic growth.

1964 Encouraged by the US state department, the army takes over and the long period of military rule begins.

1982 Brazil halts payment of its huge foreign debt.

1984 The Landless Workers' Movement (MST) begins winning land by illegally occupying unused areas.

1985 The military allows a civilian president to rule, but he is not directly elected.

1989 Fernando Collor de Mello becomes the first freely elected president, and Brazilian government enters a new era of super-corruption.

1992 Collor resigns amid corruption and an impeachment scandal. During his curtailed presidency, close to US$1 billion disappears overseas, much of it linked to drugs and arms deals.

1994 Fernando Henrique Cardoso becomes president.

1995 Seven million acres of Amazon forest are cleared in 12 months.

1997 Some 1,500 peasants march 1,200km (746 miles) to Brasilia demonstrating for land reform.

1998 Cardoso is re-elected. The economy is in a mess.

2000 Brazil celebrates its 500th anniversary, but indigenous Indians protest. Their population, once 5–10 million, is now just 350,000. Maria do Carmo Jeronimo dies, aged 129. She was born as a slave in Minas Gerais in 1871, and achieved her dream of seeing the ocean when she was 127 years old.

2002 The MST occupies President Cardoso's family ranch. Brazil wins its fifth football World Cup. Lula, after four failed attempts, is elected president.

2003 Police free about 800 slaves from a farm in Bahia. 25,000 Brazilians are thought to still work as slaves, mostly for loggers and ranchers in remote Amazon areas.

2005 When 30 people are killed in a premeditated massacre in Rio, the finger of suspicion is pointed at rogue police. A referendum rejects a ban on gun sales. The Workers Party is shaken by corruption scandals and resignations. In London, an innocent Brazilian electrician, Jean Charles de Menezes, is shot in the head seven times by anti-terrorist police.

2006 In a close-fought contest, Lula is elected to a second term as president.

2007 A Slovenian, Martin Strel, becomes the first man to swim the length of the Amazon, completing the 5,265-km (3,272-mile) marathon in 66 days. After Colombia drops out, Brazil becomes the only country in the running to host football's 2014 World Cup.

2020 Deforestation of the Amazon is expected to reach 30–40 per cent.

Politics

Around 1.5 million people travel on the London Underground every day. They get up, go to work, and go home to a hot meal and a warm bed. Many of them seem unhappy; a smile is a rare thing on a tube train. Fill those trains for a fortnight, and that is the number of people who are starving in Brazil – around 44 million souls. Close to five million rural families are homeless and have no land to work. If they are lucky, they toil in company plantations for one meal a day. Meanwhile the cities are blighted by violence, overcrowding and underfunding.

Brazilians are realists; there is always the beach and football, so they live for today and have fun. This is the image that many people have of the country, and in many respects it is true. After all, Brazilians put up with 21 years of military rule, which only ended in 1985, but now the tide is turning and this young, enormous democracy is finding its voice and flexing its muscles.

Fernando's gift

Lula, the partisan flag-bearer of the country's poor, was elected president in 2002. Yet in many respects the man behind this new power, Fernando Collor, is the workers' greatest enemy. So corrupt was his spell at the helm, so mired in the dirty politics of the rich, that even Brazilians could not tolerate it. His financier Paulo César Farias amassed close to one billion US dollars and Collor, who escaped imprisonment, is leading the high life to this day. Having rid themselves of the country's first freely elected president in 1992 the people were emboldened, yet not enough to elect one of their own. Perhaps Lula, hardly the statesman, reminded them too much of themselves. It would be another ten years before Lula and the Workers' Party took control.

Zero Hunger

One of Lula's most important programmes is 'Zero Hunger', aimed at eradicating the starvation and extreme poverty that is Brazil's shame. Food and vitamins are distributed to those in most need and unused lands are parcelled out to the homeless (*see 'Lula and the landless', pp106–7*). The Bolsa Familia (Family Grant) is another success. Poor parents are given a small monthly allowance; in return they must vaccinate their children and keep them in school. These programmes directly benefit the 11 million families that Lula promised to feed.

Looking ahead

The Workers' Party does not pretend this is a long-term solution, but opposition politicians are fierce in their criticism, highlighting individual cases of malnutrition. These are the same politicians who have spent decades getting rich off the backs of the poor, as their fathers and grandfathers did before them. One such politician is Augusto Farias, brother of Paulo César Farias. In 2003, he was a congressman in Brazil's parliament when police found 141 slaves in his enormous ranch in the northeast. Disease-ridden, regularly beaten and fed nothing but scraps, they had been tricked into a life of debt servitude. Such politicians and their wealthy backers have a lot to lose if the poor begin to demand their human rights.

The fate of the huge population is decided in the ivory towers of Brazil's National Congress

Culture

'Without samba, there is an emptiness that would never be filled. It's a pill for our sickness, a medicine for the heart. There is no substitute…Take away the samba and we're nobody.' *(Carlos Cachaùa, composer).*

Brazil comes with an unforgettable soundtrack – eminently likeable and frequently electrifying – and almost always accompanied by dance. For Brazilians, music is the ultimate expression of their nature, as well as of their history and culture; it is sexual, emotional, religious and political, one of the country's most successful exports and a true national treasure.

A combination of indigenous roots, African rhythms and Portuguese lyricism, nowhere is Brazil's rich cultural mix more obvious than in its music. It is inseparable from its political history and the core of its culture; this is the only country in the world where its most popular musician (Gilberto Gil) is also Minister of Culture. Both Gil and songwriter Caetano Veloso, who together invented the experimental musical form Tropicalism in the 1960s, were imprisoned and exiled during the military dictatorship.

Invocation to the gods

The freed slaves from Bahia made homes in Rio's *favelas* in the late 19th century, and created samba, which comes from the Angolan word *semba*, an invocation to the gods. For the Africans in Brazil, samba was a celebration of their heritage and religious worship, but it was initially banned as obscene. When it began to be used with percussion at carnival, the dictator Vargas used it to present a vision of racial – and social – harmony, paying government subsidies to samba schools that put on patriotic performances.

Great party

Like samba, *forró* is a festivity turned musical style, its name coming from *forró bodó*, meaning 'great party'. The infectious accordion-driven sound is the celebratory music of the northeast and the region's most popular dance form. *Forró* dates back to the late 19th century when cowboys of this parched area celebrated the end of the dry season, and it reached national popularity in the 1950s.

New Wave

In the late 1950s, composer Antonio Carlos Jobim and guitarist João Gilberto were captivated by the 'cool jazz' coming out of the United States and, in true Brazilian musical tradition, fused it with samba rhythms, making it even smoother. The result was Bossa Nova, meaning 'New Wave', which quickly became the intellectual's music of choice and went on to rival samba as the national rhythm. Bossa Nova is still one of the dominant musical forms in Brazil and popular throughout the world.

Good vibrations

Musica Popular Brasileira (Brazilian Popular Music or MPB) is a blanket phrase that describes all movements in Brazilian music after Bossa Nova, embracing everything from smooth jazz to bad pop. It includes everything from the monotonous and aggressive Lambada dance craze of the late '80s to *axé*, an African-pop-rock fusion that hit Brazil in the '90s and means 'good vibration'.

A TOP TEN OF BRAZILIAN MUSICIANS

Daniela Mercury
Bebel Gilberto
Marisa Monte
Gilberto Gil
João Gilberto
Antonio Carlos Jobim
Caetano Veloso
Maria Bethania
Tom Jobim
Chico Buarque

A carnival queen spreads her wings

The beautiful people

Brazilian women are known the world over for being exquisite, not least because their svelte, semi-naked figures are projected around the globe annually during carnival. But many find this stereotypical image of Brazilian beauty frustrating and belittling. Beauty in Brazil is certainly not skin-deep; showing your shapely stomach in the street or having a bulbous bottom is not so much provocative as celebratory. Brazilians take a rounded view.

Because of love

'Tall and tanned and long and lovely…' are the most resonant of the English lyrics of *The Girl from Ipanema*. In the Portuguese version, however, the emphasis is on her overall loveliness and the 'sweet swing' of the hips of the girl who is 'more than a poem, the most beautiful thing I have ever seen'. She has become more gorgeous, as the chorus goes, 'Because of love. Because of love. Because of love'.

Two-faced

You would be hard-pressed to find a black face in *Caras*, Brazil's answer to *Hello* magazine, yet the country has the largest black population in the western hemisphere. The publishers argue that the magazine is a reflection of Brazilian high society, but the media manage to present a Caucasian face even to Salvador's carnival where around 99 per cent of revellers are Afro-Caribbean. Many visitors confuse the presence of 100 different colours of skin with equality, but race defines Brazil's brutal class-ridden society, with the blackest at the bottom of the pile.

Plastic people

Brazil has one of the highest plastic surgery rates in the world and has been regarded as the international leader for decades. But in Brazil it is seen as a human right; surgeons provide subsidised or even free operations for the poor, and anyone can get plastic surgery on HP. This is a country where octogenarians regularly go under the knife, skinny 18-year-old boys get tummy tucks and supplies of silicone sell out every year in the run-up to carnival.

Open up

Some of the most sensuous people on the planet live in Brazil, but it is not just about sexuality. Many Europeans are perceived as *fechado* (closed).

Brazilians will happily cavort continuously for five days and nights at carnival, and find the European 'fear to enjoy themselves', even while drunk, totally unfathomable. The vast majority of Brazilians have nothing, but have made celebration into an art form.

Simply divine

The beautiful Brazilian people have an uplifting spirituality that goes to the very heart of the nation, inseparable from their continued survival and enduring appeal. Anyone who has made friends with someone from a *favela* or with a child on the street in Brazil won't forget their all-engulfing positive attitude. You only have to compare the thousand-dollar boxes at carnival full of rich white people, with the beaming and largely black performers from the *favela* below, to see who is having the most fun.

The beautiful people congregate on the beach

Festivals and events

In many ways Brazil is a celebration; music and dancing are never far away. Even those festivities that revolve around the Catholic calendar somehow contrive to be hedonistic. ***Carnaval*** *(carnival) is of course the main event and takes place all over the country in some form* (see pp94–5)*. Officially beginning in February or March, the whole period from Christmas is a build-up to the explosive celebrations that go on for the best part of a week.*

Countrywide

Revellers all over Brazil dress up in white for **Reveillon** (New Year's Eve) to pay homage to Iemanjá, the goddess of water. Rio, particularly Copacabana beach, is the focus for celebrations where several million people gather for a unique spectacle that combines Candomblé offerings and candles with live music and fireworks.

Festa Junina (June Festival) takes place in Brazil's mid-winter, mostly in the northeast but throughout the country. The feasts of St John, St Anthony and St Peter occur on different days in June, culminating in a month-long celebration. This is very much a rural festival, with traditional food, clothing and dance (particularly *quadrilha*, a kind of square dancing).

Predictably, the country's most conservative festivities are the traditional **Semana Santa** religious parades and military parades to mark **Independence Day** (7 September) and **Republic Day** (15 November).

Rio and the south

Brazil boasts more Grand Prix winners than any other country, making São Paulo a fitting host for the annual **Grand Prix** (*www.formula1.com*) every September or October. The city also puts on the **São Paulo Bienal**, Latin America's biggest art event, every even-numbered year in Oscar Niemeyer's modernist pavilion in Ibirapuera Park.

The **Festa Literária Internacional de Paraty** (Paraty International Literary Festival, *www.flip.org.br*) is another new but important date on the international arts calendar (*see 'Paraty', p52*).

Oktoberfest in Blumenau is a nod to the south's German roots, when for 17 days every October, a decidedly young crowd gorges on bratwurst sandwiches and beer.

Salvador and surrounds

Between December and March, the city of Salvador is a riot of festivals, both religious and folk, with singing and dancing and fascinating rituals. The **Lavagem do Bonfim** takes place the second Thursday of January when a lively *cortejo* (procession) with music from carnival groups such as Filhos de Gandhy (Sons of Gandhi) and Olodum makes its way from the Church of Conceição da Praia to the Church of Bonfim, for its ritual washing. On 2 February, offerings of flowers and jewellery are made alongside music and celebrations at Salvador's Praia Vermelha in the **Festa of Iemanjá**.

The northeast and the Amazon

Deeply rooted in the rural tradition, **Bumba Meu Boi** is an exuberant folklore dance and parade of characters including the ox, around which the festival is based. São Luís in the northeast hosts events in mid-June to mid-August, while Parintins in Amazonas puts on a three-day extravaganza with floats and singing and dancing centred around the Bumbódromo (Parintins' answer to Rio's Sambódromo), which is fast becoming a significant tourist event.

A spectacular carnival costume

Highlights

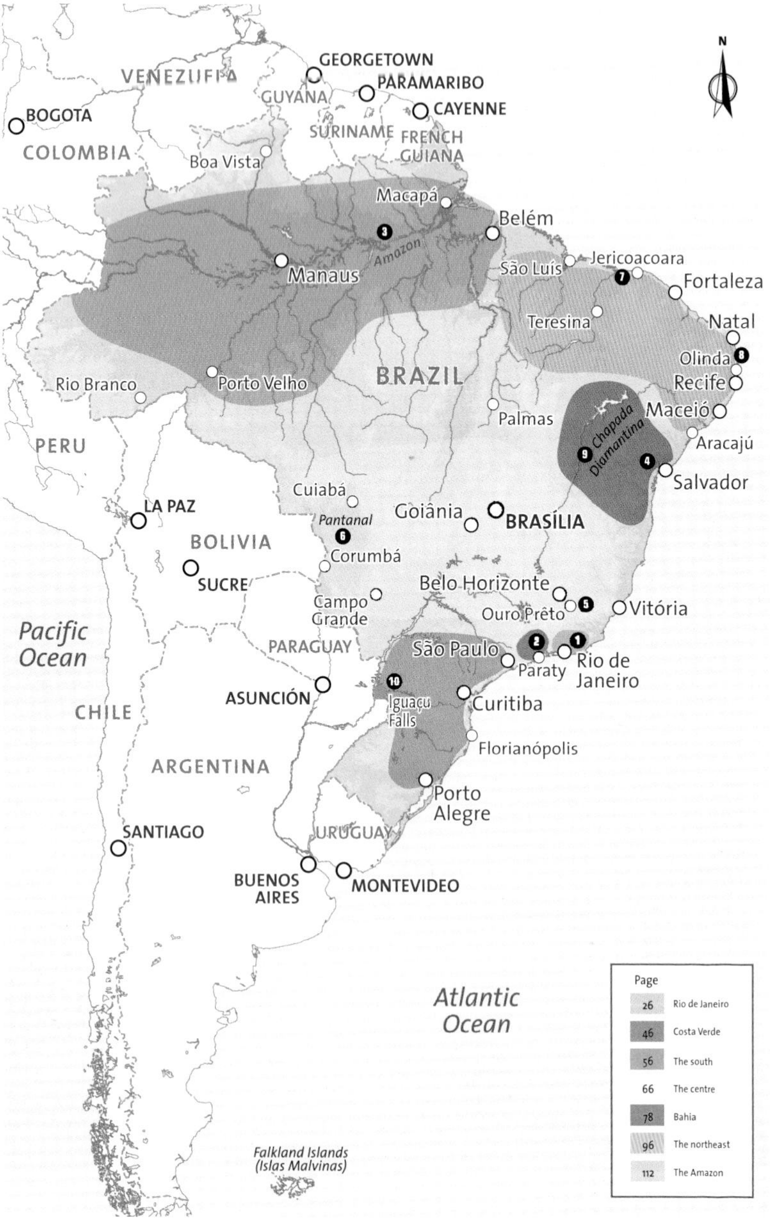
N
GEORGETOWN
VENEZUELA
PARAMARIBO
GUYANA
CAYENNE
BOGOTA
SURINAME
FRENCH GUIANA
COLOMBIA
Boa Vista
Macapá
Belém
3
Amazon
Manaus
São Luís
Jericoacoara
7
Fortaleza
Teresina
Natal
Olinda
8
Recife
Rio Branco
Porto Velho
BRAZIL
Palmas
Chapada Diamantina
Maceió
9
4
Aracajú
PERU
Salvador
Cuiabá
LA PAZ
Goiânia
BRASÍLIA
Pantanal
6
BOLIVIA
Corumbá
SUCRE
Belo Horizonte
Campo Grande
5
Ouro Prêto
Vitória
Pacific Ocean
PARAGUAY
São Paulo
2
1
Paraty
Rio de Janeiro
ASUNCIÓN
10
Iguaçu Falls
Curitiba
CHILE
Florianópolis
ARGENTINA
Porto Alegre
SANTIAGO
URUGUAY
BUENOS AIRES
MONTEVIDEO
Atlantic Ocean
Falkland Islands (Islas Malvinas)
Page
26 Rio de Janeiro
46 Costa Verde
56 The south
66 The centre
78 Bahia
96 The northeast
112 The Amazon

❶ **Rio de Janeiro** Lie on the beach and soak up one of the most glorious cities in the world.

❷ **Paraty** Stroll colonial cobbled streets and take to the turquoise waters of the bay.

❸ **The Amazon** Take a boat up this extraordinary river through dense jungle teeming with animal life.

❹ **Salvador** Absorb the African soul of Brazil's historic and most electrifying city.

❺ **Ouro Preto** Marvel at the baroque splendour of this colonial gem, where time has stood still since the end of the gold rush.

❻ **Pantanal** Spot giant guinea pigs and enormous cats in this open-air wildlife reserve.

❼ **Jericoacoara** Wind down on one of the world's most beautiful beaches.

❽ **Olinda** Breathe in the atmosphere of its pretty colonial streets and churches.

❾ **Chapada Diamantina** Hike through the spectacular natural beauty of Brazil's 'Lost World'.

❿ **Iguaçu Falls** Feel the spray on your face from one of the largest waterfalls on the planet.

Sunset in Rio de Janeiro

Suggested itineraries

Brazil is big – very big. Allow plenty of time to enjoy the country that is almost the size of a continent. The relaxed way of life calls for some laid-back scheduling. Some packages cram in as many 'sights' as physically possible but don't necessarily make for the most enjoyable holiday. Your best memories of Brazil are likely to be as much to do with its people as its natural wonders, so don't try to see everything. Either confine yourself to one region, or be prepared for some extensive air travel; luckily there are some bargain internal flights to be had. Bus journeys, even between major cities, can last up to two days.

Take things at your own pace

In Brazil life is, quite simply, a beach. Any itinerary will take in one or probably several of them, and they are undeniably Brazil's main attraction. All of the major tourist cities have stretches of sand, but the prettiest are, inevitably, out of the main urban areas and need time to get to.

A long weekend

A long weekend in Brazil is within even Europeans' reach, thanks to charter flights to the northeast of the country, with bargain fares and flying time of little more than eight hours. Fly to Salvador and enjoy two days in the city, with trips to the nearby bay and beaches. Or spend a bit more and revel in the city of Rio with all it has to offer.

A week

A week gives visitors the chance to fully experience one of these beautiful cities – or even both – with time for some serious relaxation. Or, combine either city with a quick trip to the Amazon, a two-day trip to Iguaçu or a whirlwind tour of the country's colonial cities.

Two or three weeks

Two weeks is enough time to sample your point of arrival, whether Rio, Salvador or São Paulo, together with some exotic wildlife-watching in the

Sample Salvador on a long weekend

Pantanal or the Amazon. Alternatively, take a hedonist's view and spend most of your time on the easily accessible beaches, learning a little of the country's rich history via forays into cities and colonial towns.

In three weeks, you can see most of Brazil's highlights. As an example, land in Rio, spending seven days in the country's – if not the world's – most exciting city, before taking a short flight up to Salvador. Enjoy its beaches and distinct Afro-centric culture before making your way up to one of the last great wildernesses on the planet: the Amazon.

Longer

A month in Brazil allows you to see some key sights and indulge your specialist interests, whether it is colonial history, wildlife-watching or music. If you want the maximum Carnaval experience, the three main centres of the greatest celebration on earth can be sampled even in a week; land in Rio and after three days fly to Salvador for a very different African experience, before travelling up to Recife and Olinda. Whatever your timescale, don't miss the chance to travel into the interior, to get to the heart of Brazil, both spiritually and geographically.

Rio de Janeiro

'Oh, I'd love to roll to Rio. Some day before I'm old!' *(Rudyard Kipling,* The Beginning of the Armadillos: Just So Stories, *1902).*

Rio de Janeiro was named when the enormous bay of Guanabara was mistaken for a river by Portuguese explorer Pedro Cabral in January 1502. The magnetic city that attracts more visitors than anywhere else in Brazil is often also confused for the capital, even though it relinquished that title in 1960. The fact is that Rio is physically extraordinary and its mix of mountains, lakes, forest, ocean and white-sand beaches makes it one of the most beautiful cities in the world.

The city has a special spirit too, projecting glamour and squalor in equal measures. Between the 1920s and 1950s, in what was the city's heyday, international stars came to play and Fred Astaire and Ginger Rogers 'flew down to Rio' in 1933. While Copacabana is living off its glory days,

The extraordinary beach city of Rio

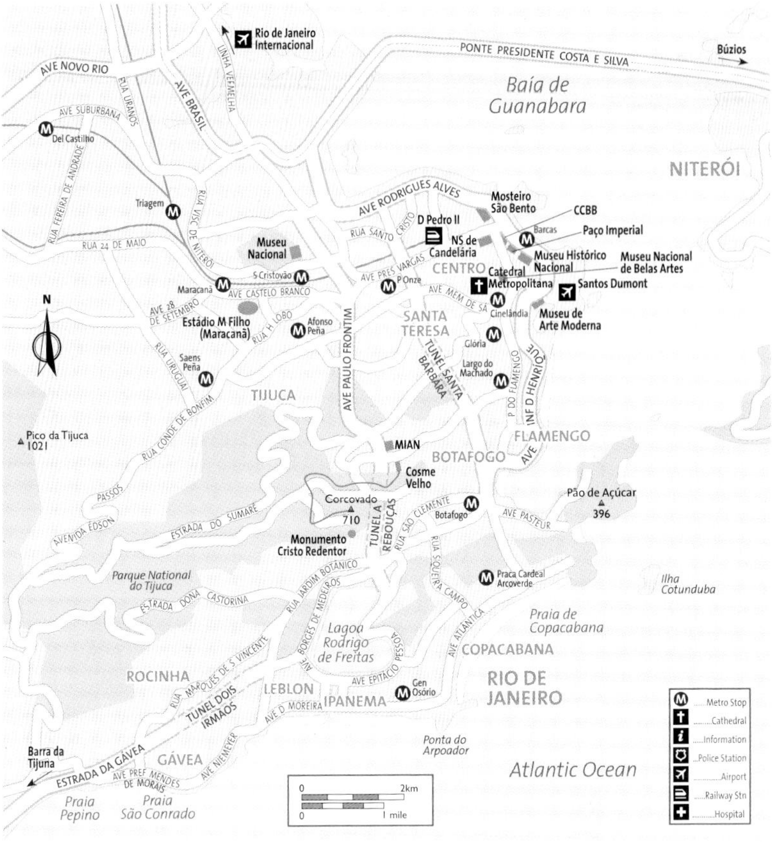

today Ipanema is where the beautiful people go.

Santa Teresa, once a no-go area, is now a thriving artistic neighbourhood on a hill in the style of Montmartre, an exciting place to visit day or night. The city's *favelas* are the most noticeable of any in Brazil, perched high on *morros* in central locations. They are infamous for drugs and violence, but are also home to much of the city's workforce and the hub of its creative energy.

While Rio's main draws are its natural wonders, it is also Brazil's 'cultural corridor'; many of the country's best museums, art galleries and cultural centres are found here. Such a star attraction is the city, along with its residents, the *cariocas*, that it is easy to forget Rio is a state too, with the chic resort of Búzios and the imperial city of Petrópolis providing cool seaside and mountain retreats.

COPACABANA AND IPANEMA

These two beaches are the very essence of Rio, where *cariocas* live, love and play. A visit to either Copacabana or Ipanema means so much more than just sunbathing; these twin stretches of sand are the heart and the soul of the city, acting as office, pub and playground. If Copacabana is the older, slightly scruffy sibling, Ipanema is its younger, prettier sister, with better restaurants, boutiques and beautiful people.

Stake a claim to your own little part of the beach, hire an umbrella and beach chair from one of the stalls on the sand, and maybe have a massage. Along the road, try a beer, sandwich, or *mate* (Brazilian iced tea), or ideally a hydrating *água de coco* (coconut water). The vendor will cut a hole for a straw in the iced coconut; when it's empty, bring the nut back and he will chop it up and give you a section of the shell for you to scrape out the nutritious flesh.

Copacabana

Running for 4km (2½ miles) between Leme and the fort, this beach is known for its 5-star hotels, granddads on the beach, transvestites and, at night at least, prostitutes. Copacabana is generally cheaper than Ipanema for food, drinks and apartments, although not necessarily hotels. The icing-white Copacabana Palace (1923) – the first building on the whole beach and the scene for the film *Flying Down to Rio* starring Fred Astaire and Ginger Rogers – still stands sentinel in its centre.

INSIDER INFORMATION

Both beaches are now floodlit at night, but still, stay safe and take precautions against theft at all times. Don't take belongings other than a towel and enough money for the beach. If you are desperate for photos, take a few shots and then return your camera to the hotel before going back to the beach for the rest of the day.

Posing for the camera in Ipanema

Ipanema

This beach runs for 6km (3¾ miles), including Leblon to the west. The name means 'dangerous waters' because of the current, so take heed of the big waves and strong undertow. There is something for everyone here: Baixo Bebé is a nursery/playground at the Leblon end, while Posto 8 is where any self-respecting gay man in trunks takes himself. On Sundays, the oceanside lane is closed to traffic; watch out instead for cyclists and roller skaters.

Leaning left

Ipanema is egalitarian in many ways. The Republic of Ipanema, also known as the Cemetério dos Elefantes (Cemetery of the Elephants), was, in the '50s and '60s, a haven for intellectuals from the whole of South America. Many of the real hippies may be long gone, but the admittedly touristy Feira Hippie (hippy market) on Sundays continues (8am–midnight) on Praça General Osório one block back from the seafront, with jewellery, handicrafts and furniture.

After hours

Applause fills the air at Ponta do Arpoador at the Copacabana end of Ipanema, where locals and tourists gather to watch the sunsets that often colour the sky a glorious pink. Many then head for sundowners at the *Garota de Ipanema* (Girl from Ipanema) bar at Rua de Vinícius de Moraes, or to the gay-friendly *Bofetada* at Rua Farme de Amoedo, both just a few blocks back from the beach.

Crowds at play in Copacabana

Rio's billion-dollar zoo

In the alphabetical Brazilian menagerie, 'a' is for avestruz (ostrich), 'b' is for burro (donkey), and so it goes on, but it is animal numbers, not letters, that occupy the dreams of hopeful *cariocas*. Every day millions of them take part in an illegal lottery where the numbers 1 to 4 are represented by the ostrich, 5 to 8 by the donkey, and so on, all the way through the alphabet and up to 100. This is Jogo do Bicho (Animal Game) and it is very big business. When it comes time to pick an animal, Rio's residents take their inspiration from daily life and their imagination. When a butterfly lands on a driver's windshield, it must be a sign. If thirsty dreams are spent wandering the desert, rush out and bet on the camel.

It all began in Rio's real-life zoo over a hundred years ago. Visitor numbers were down, and so one bright spark introduced a raffle. Each entry ticket had the image of an animal, and the winning ticket won a cash prize. From those humble beginnings, the game has grown into a huge industry controlled by criminal barons known as *bicheiros*. On over 3,000 street corners throughout Rio, ramshackle *pontos* (betting stands) attract people from all walks of life, hoping to make a killing on the horses, or peacocks.

Money talks

The biggest open secret in Brazil is that Carnaval is funded by the *bicheiros*. Each of the samba schools is a huge operation, training dancers and drummers throughout the year, building floats, sewing costumes and working towards their night in the Sambódromo. They are rooted in Rio's *favela* communities, rich in talent, but financially bereft. In return for funding, the *bicheiros* control Carnaval behind the scenes, and even act as judges.

Rumours of bias and under-the-table deals to secure promotion to Grupo Especial, Carnaval's 'premier league', cannot be substantiated but are generally believed to be true. In recent years, the government has tried to build up legitimate sponsorship, but most estimates, even now, suggest that the funding split is 50-50 at best. After securing promotion in 2006, Rio's oldest samba school, Estácio de Sá, opened Carnaval 2007, with leggy dancers in skimpy Aztec costumes and a gigantic float emblazoned with their emblematic lion's head.

All the schools are desperate to stay in the Especial. Lower groups do not parade in the Sambódromo, but in the neighbouring streets, which means less television coverage and less sponsorship, legitimate or otherwise. In recent Carnavals, parades had begun to run over with dancers struggling in heavy costumes under the hot morning sun. As a result, organisers cut the number of schools allowed to parade in the Sambódromo from 12 to 10, making the Especial even more difficult to get into and remain in.

Bingo or Bocho

At the moment, there is not much choice for Brazilians who like a flutter; casinos are illegal here. This partly explains why an estimated ten million Jogo do Bicho bets are placed each day throughout Brazil. In Rio alone, there are over 80,000 people employed in the industry, which produces a winner each evening. That may change with the government considering alterations to the casino laws, but for the moment, Carnaval, gambling and gang bosses continue to be inextricably linked.

The Animal Game funds the spectacle of Carnaval

PÃO DE AÇÚCAR AND CRISTO REDENTOR

The squashed cone of the Sugarloaf and the outstretched arms of Christ the Redeemer are the two enduring images of Rio. Both can appear as if by magic at locations throughout the city, and the views from their mountaintops are not to be missed. The city is often shrouded in a thick mist, when an ascent of either summit is almost pointless, so pick your day for a visit very carefully.

INSIDER INFORMATION

Rio's two most popular attractions tend to be crowded mid-morning and mid-afternoon. The best time to arrive is half an hour before sunset; see the city glow in the orange sun, then, as night falls, watch it sparkle. Both attractions have shops, cafés and disabled access. Avoid the unnecessarily extravagant helicopter rides which do untold damage to the environment on their short spins around the peaks. And be aware that it is not necessary to go as part of a guided tour to either sight; taxis are very reasonable and will wait for as long as you want – just agree a fixed price beforehand.

Pão de Açúcar

Visitors must take not one but two lurching James Bond-style cable cars to reach the summit. The first travels 220m (722ft) up from the beach of Praia Vermelha, offering a bird's-eye view of Botafogo and the bay of Guanabara. The second car takes passengers up another 396m (1,300ft) for spectacular, panoramic views of the city and across to Niterói.

If you'd rather hike, the pathway of Pista Cláudio Coutinho etched into the base of the granite 'loaf' offers a wonderful walk between the wide-open sea and dense rainforest filled with passionflowers. It is even possible to climb the sheer cliff, following the Caminho da Costa, which reaches all the way to the Sugarloaf summit; there are other climbs of various degrees of difficulty off the main path.

Cable car. Avenida Pasteur 520, Urca. Tel: (21) 2546 8400. www.bondinho.com.br. Open: 8am–9pm, ticket office closes 7.50pm. Admission charge.

Christ looks across to Sugarloaf

Cristo Redentor

Standing atop the Corcovado (Hunchback) mountain which rises a sheer 710m (2,330ft) out of the earth, the 30-m (98-ft) tall statue of Christ can be seen by office workers, *favela* dwellers and penthouse owners alike. The figure appears to embrace Rio's residents, as if offering some kind of abiding hope in this violence-filled city.

The best way to get there is by train (sit on the right-hand side for the best views), which leaves every half hour from Cosme Velho station. At the end of the train line, 220 steep steps lead to the summit, with three lifts and two escalators providing alternative means to the top. At the feet of Christ, there are 360-degree views of the city and its beaches, with pictogram signs identifying key points of interest.

Rua Cosme Velho 513. Tel: (21) 2558 1329. www.corcovado.com.br. Open: 8.30am–6.30pm. Admission charge.

Museu Internacional de Arte Naif do Brasil (MIAN)

Less than a minute's walk from the Cosme Velho train station is one of the most important museums of naïve art in the world, the MIAN, with more than 6,000 works from more than 100 countries. Even if you just want to fill in some time while waiting for your train, this museum is well worth a visit.

Rua Cosme Velho 561. Tel: (21) 2205 8612. www.museunaif.com.br. Open: Wed–Sat 10am–6pm. Admission charge.

Half way to the top of the mountain

Walk: Day and night in Santa Teresa

Perched on a green hilltop high above the centre, Santa Teresa is a relaxed and bohemian enclave. Every day, jam-packed historic trams bring workers from here down to the city, returning with visitors (and cariocas *too) on their way to sample Santa Teresa's bars, restaurants and cultural centres.*

Begin your journey at the Catedral Metropolitana on the edge of Lapa.

1 Catedral Metropolitana

The walk starts at the cavernous upside-down coffee cup that is Rio's modern cathedral, but stop inside for a look at the impressive stained-glass windows.

Avenida República do Chile 245, Lapa. Head east along Chile and turn right after 200m (220yds) onto Rua Lélio Gama, where you'll find the tram terminus.

2 Bondinho (Little Tram)

Far and away the most enjoyable way to reach Santa Teresa is by tram. On Saturdays at 10am (and sometimes 2pm) there is tour guide on board to give a potted history of the city. The tram rides over the whitewashed Aqueducto de Carioca, which used to bring river water into the city centre.

Ask a local to let you know when the tram reaches Largo do Curvelo in Santa Teresa. Walk east along Rua Dias de Barros, and after 200m (220yds) take the first left onto Murtinho Nobre.

3 Museu da Chácara do Céu (Museum in the Sky)

During the 2006 Carnaval, thieves stormed this museum and stole works by Picasso, Dalí, Matisse and Monet. Happily, some works by these artists are still on display.

Murtinho Nobre 93.
Tel: (21) 2224 8891.
www.museuscastromaya.com.br.
Open: Wed–Mon noon–5pm.
Admission charge.
Return the way you came to Curvelo, and continue up, following the tram line for another 400m (440yds).

4 Largo dos Guimarães

The heart of the whole neighbourhood is this triangular plaza, where locals watch the world go by. At this height, the air is cooler than in the city below.

Walk northeast along Rua Castro, veer left into Rua Carlos Brant and walk to the tram museum (two minutes from the plaza).

5 Museu do Bonde

Scale models of old trams, a photo history and even a real tram from 1907 are on show here.

Rua Carlos Brant 14. Tel: (21) 2242 2354. Open 9am–4.30pm. Admission charge.

Head back to the plaza and walk east along Rua Almirante. ***Espirito Santa*** *(*see 'Directory', p163*), with an outdoor table overlooking the valley, is a great place for a long lazy lunch.*

6 Shopping and sundowners

Spend the afternoon wandering around the craft shops that surround Guimarães. Come sundown, one of the neighbourhood bars will probably be hosting live music; take your pick.

7 The high life

Head back down to Lapa at around 11pm for live music in Bar Semente and Rio Scenarium (*see 'Directory', p164*).

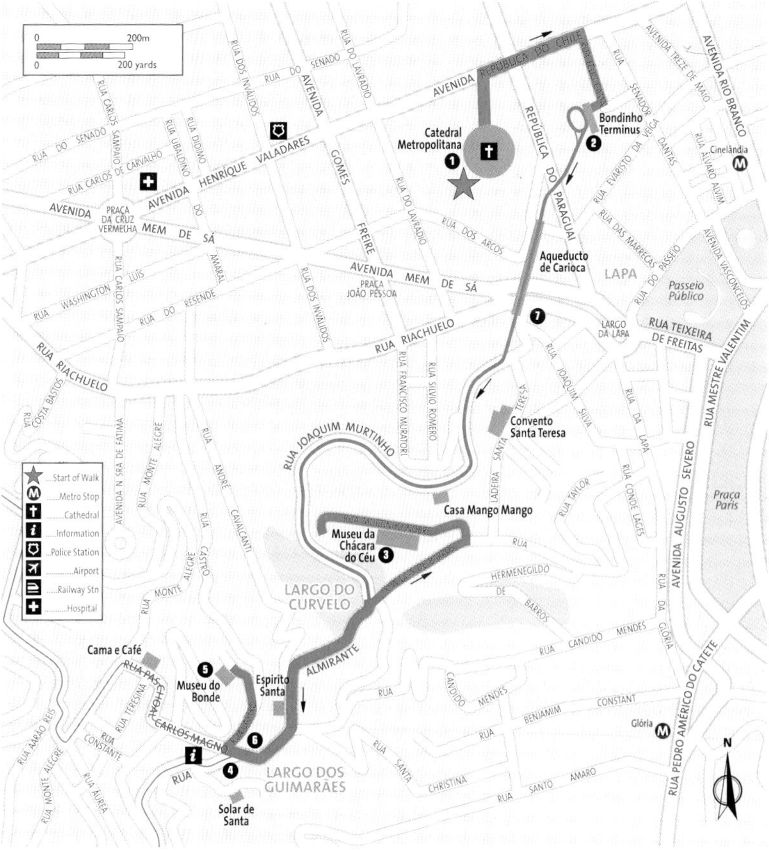

CENTRO

Centro is the birthplace of the city, offering glimpses of the past in its colonial churches and historic buildings. Although some are crumbling, they are alive as places of worship, while new life has been breathed into others that now function as cultural centres. The heart of this area is the square of Praça XV de Novembro, named after the date that the Brazilian republic was proclaimed in 1889. More recent cultural offerings can be found in the area's art museums, which are some of the best in the country. Today, the centre is Rio's business district, throbbing with office workers on weekdays and

Nossa Senhora da Candelária is Rio's largest colonial church

almost deserted in the evenings and at weekends.

Centro Cultural do Banco do Brasil (CCBB)

The 100-year-old building was the HQ of the Bank of Brazil until the bank moved to Brasilia in the 1960s, when the vacated domed building was beautifully – and expensively – restored. Today it is a 'living room' of experimental and classical art, with a cinema and eight exhibition halls.

Rua Primeiro de Março 66. Tel: (21) 2808 2020. www.bb.com.br/cultura. Open: Tue–Sun noon–8pm. Admission charge.

Churches

Igreja Nossa Senhora da Candelária

Work on the church, designed in the shape of a Latin cross, was begun in 1775. The impressive white building is lined with marble and features intricate bronze doors that were exhibited in the World Fair in Paris in 1889. Note the paintings that tell the tale of the church's early history.

Praça Pio X. Tel: (21) 2233 2324. Open: Mon–Fri 7.30am–4pm, Sat 8am–noon, Sun 9am–1pm. Free admission.

Mosteiro de São Bento

Benedictine monks founded this monastery in 1590. Perched on a hill of the same name, the UNESCO site is an oasis of peace in the middle of the city centre. Its unforgiving exterior gives way to a wonderfully over-the-top baroque interior, which is filled with ecstatic Gregorian chants on Sundays.

Rua Dom Gerardo 68. Tel: (21) 2206 8100. www.osb.org.br. Open: 7am–noon & 2–6pm. Free admission.

Museums

Museu de Arte Moderna (MAM)

This suitably contemporary building of concrete and glass houses a significant collection of Brazilian modern art, including film and sculpture.

Avenida Infante Dom Henrique 85. Tel: (21) 2240 4944. www.mamrio.org.br. Open: Tue–Sat noon–6pm, Sun noon–7pm. Admission charge.

Museu Nacional de Belas Artes

Inspired by the Louvre, this national museum of fine art specialises in 18th-, 19th- and early 20th-century paintings, sculpture and furniture from Europe and Brazil. The building dating from 1908 is one of the star attractions, along with works by Frans Post, Brazil's first landscape painter.

Avenida Rio Branco 199. Tel: (21) 2240 0068. www.mnba.gov.br (Portuguese only). Open: Tue–Fri 10am–6pm, Sat 1–6pm. Admission charge.

Paço Imperial (Imperial Palace)

Built in 1743, this was the seat of the Portuguese viceroys and the town palace of the emperor. It is now one of the best-preserved buildings in Rio and an important cultural centre.

Praca XV de Novembro 48. Tel: (21) 2533 4491. www.pacoimperial.com.br. Open: Tue–Sun noon–6pm. Admission charge.

A girl from the *favela*

The bar where the bossa nova hit *The Girl from Ipanema* was written is full of tourists these days. Isabella Pereira works a couple of blocks away; she is young, pretty and lives in a flat with stunning views of Rio's seafront. But her home is not a beachside penthouse; Isabella lives in Rocinha, the largest *favela* in the world. Most people call it a 'slum', but for Isabella it is a *comunidade* (community). Her boss is the wife of a Rio businessman, one of many who trust the *favelados* to clean their homes, cook their meals and mind their children.

Highs and lows

Favelas exist all over Brazil, but in Rio the juxtaposition is incongruous. Four million people – a third of the city's population – live in shacks high up in the cool hills, overlooking the rich who scurry around the sterile asphalt below. In the 1970s, driven by hunger and unemployment, Isabella's father left the northeast to work in Rio's construction boom. He moved to a temporary workers' camp on unused land near the building sites; the camp became permanent and Rocinha is now one of 600 sprawling *favelas* in the city.

See no evil...

People from the *favelas* do most of the city's 'dirty work' – everything from cleaning the streets to waiting at the best restaurants – yet there are no

Children flying kites in a Rio *favela*

road signs pointing the way home for Isabella, and Rocinha is not even shown on maps. Deprived of basic services, the maze-like alleyways are strewn with rubbish and soaked in sewage. Isabella's birth does not appear on city records, and her neighbour, who runs a bar, pays protection money to the police, militia or gangsters, depending on who is running the show that month.

Moral majority

When violence and drugs hit the headlines, or even when poverty and promiscuity are discussed, fingers point at the *favelas*. According to Isabella, 'People in the rich parts of the city employ us as maids and nannies, but they don't even treat us as human. My family are very religious, I don't drink or smoke, and my father works 14 hours a day, seven days a week. It is the rich people who buy most of the cocaine from the drug gangs, not us.'

DROPPING IN

An unaccompanied visit to a *favela* is asking for trouble, but avoid commercial tours that offer no insight into local life. Try to visit, but with an organisation that benefits local communities, or talk to your waiter, maid or shop assistant who will almost certainly be delighted to show you their home. Iko Poran (*Tel: (21) 2205 1365. www.ikoporan.org*) organises trips to some of their fascinating projects on 'positive impact' visits.

Rocinha's hillside sprawl

An inspiration

Samba was born in a *favela* in Rio and it is no exaggeration to say that Carnaval and this vibrant city would be nothing without these communities. Baile funk – a high-energy, sexual dance-rap fusion – blasts out from the hilltops and is the 24-hour soundtrack in the most popular bar in Via Ápia, Rocinha's main street. The bar is called 'The Girl from Via Ápia' in a satirical nod to the soulless bar close to Isabella's workplace.

GREEN RIO

No city in the world is quite as green as Rio. The whole urban area is, in many respects, just one enormous green space, where concrete appears to constantly battle to keep the jungle at bay. Rio has the largest urban forest in the world and the botanical gardens here are a UNESCO biosphere, sheltering birds, monkeys, insects and thousands of plant species, including the now endangered Brazilwood tree (Pau Brasil) that gave the country its name.

Parque Nacional da Tijuca

From the late 18th century, aristocratic refugees fleeing the French Revolution began to raze this pristine mountain forest, selling it off as charcoal, and planting profitable coffee trees in its stead. Rio's drinking water became polluted in the process and a distraught Emperor Pedro II ordered one of his army officers to fix things in 1861. Major Gomes Archer organised extensive replanting of the forest and it remains one of Rio's treasures to this day.

Exploring the labyrinthine forest is best done with a guide, as most of the paths are either poorly marked or not at all. Friendly English-speaking guide Paulo Celani offers thrilling open-top jeep safaris into the forest (*Tel: (21) 2268 0565. www.geocities.com/riojeeptour*). Once beneath the canopy, there is a multitude of trekking paths to choose from, some leading to hidden waterfalls, others to the remains of grand mansions from the coffee plantation days. The highest point in the forest, Pico da Tijuca, is 1,021m (3,300ft) above sea level. It is a one-hour climb, with the final stretch made via a staircase cut into the hillside.

One of Tijuca's many waterfalls

The whole of this urban forest was made a national park in 1961, and admission is free, yet Rio's residents rarely make time to visit. The forest is also home to the statue of Cristo Redentor (*see pp32–3*) which can be visited with the same jeep tours, or separately.

Open: 7am–9pm. Free admission.

Instituto Moreira Salles

Gávea is one of Rio's wealthiest neighbourhoods, but all the expensive

restaurants, bars and shops are outshone by this free cultural institute, the former home of one of Brazil's richest bankers. A peaceful and inspiring spot, with a jungle garden and waterfall, the institute exhibits itinerant sculptural works and paintings of the highest quality, both in the gardens and in the well-designed interior gallery spaces.
Rua Marquês de São Vicente 476, Gávea. Tel: (21) 3284 7400. www.ims.com.br. Open: noon–8pm. Free admission.

Jardim Botânico do Rio de Janeiro

Over 8,000 plant species grow behind the high walls of these botanical gardens, which cover 140 hectares (346 acres). The gardens were created in 1808 by Portugal's prince regent as a nursery where imported plants could become acclimatised to the Brazilian climate. A few years later, his son opened them to the public, and today they attract over 600,000 visitors every year. Since 1992, UNESCO has recognised the gardens as a biosphere reserve, and much important research is conducted here. Yet it is easy to forget the science and just wander aimlessly, listening to the birdsong and admiring the colours and shapes of the plants, with a lunchtime picnic at one of the many lush ornamental lakes.
Rua Jardim Botânico 1008. Tel: (21) 2294 6012 or (21) 3874 1214. www.jbrj.gov.br. Open: 8am–5pm. Admission charge.

Rio's botanic gardens are awash with colour

ACTIVE RIO

Perhaps the landscape invites activity or *cariocas* just live and breathe fitness, but the city just never seems to be still. The beaches of Copacabana and Ipanema have gym equipment and improvised volleyball courts, and now that they are illuminated at night, games and iron pumping continue from morning to midnight. On Sundays, when the beach road is closed to traffic, walkers, joggers and cyclists fill the tarmac.

Boat trips

Water faces you almost every way you turn in Rio; enjoy it on a boat tour, private yacht charter, or even on a pedalo. A Guanabara Bay Cruise is a classic, if touristy, way to experience the ocean, with trips leaving from Gloria Marina throughout the day. **Saveiros Tour** offers historic schooner trips that are particularly recommended (*www.saveiros.com.br*). Half-day boat tours sail around the islands of Cagarras off Ipanema, with the option to snorkel, fish or even dive.

Hang-gliding

Jump off the ramp at Pedra Bonita on a tandem flight and land at Pepino beach, São Conrado in a serene rather than stomach-lurching flight. Trips usually include transfers from and to your hotel, but flights depend on the wind, so be prepared for your flight to be postponed for several days.

Hang-gliding high above the city

A professional, calm, experienced guide is essential; Paulo Celani of **Justfly** is one of the best (*Tel: (21) 2268 0565 or (21) 9985 7540. www.justfly.com.br*).

Hiking

Parque Tijuca is the most obvious location for any serious walking; more than just the city's lungs, this is the largest urban forest in the world, and cut through with scenic waterfalls. Hire a guide as the trails are not properly marked and it is very easy to get lost. **Rio Hiking** offers half- and full-day hiking tours as well as diving, cycling and climbing trips (*www.riohiking.com.br*).

A trail around the base of Sugarloaf (*see 'Pão de Açúcar and Cristo Redentor', pp32–3*) plunges into thick rainforest right in the middle of the city.

Lakeside

The wealthy residents of Zona Sul use the calm waters of the Lagoa Rodrigo de Freitas not so much as a haven as a hive of activity. This is one of the best-equipped recreation areas in the city. Rowing boats, pedalos and even water skis can be hired to cross the fish-filled, freshwater lake, which is not clean enough to swim in. Cyclists and joggers fight for space on the 7-km ($4^1/_3$-mile) track that circles the lake, surrounded by the trees of Parque Tom Jobim. Nearby, tennis players thrash it out on open-air courts, and roller skaters spin on a purpose-built rink.

Heading into the surf

Surfing

Rio's beaches have the best waves in winter, which is good for surfers as this is when there are the fewest tourists. Even so, at this time, Ipanema and Copacabana, and Arpoador in the middle, can still have too many swimmers for comfort. The best spots to head for are on the edge of the city; the pretty little beach of Prainha, north of Barra da Tijuca, is *the* surfers' beach and consistently has the best waves. The Surf Bus (*www.surfbus.com.br, Portuguese only*) operates daily 7am–7pm, taking surfers and their boards to 11 beaches between Botafogo and Prainha and also has a surf school for novices.

BÚZIOS

This 8-km (5-mile) long peninsula is a skinny, scalloped stretch of land with lovely, small beaches, rocky islands and secret coves. Brazilians tend to rave about Búzios and its rustic charm, but this popular destination for wealthy Argentines, Brazilian celebrities and international tourists is not for everyone. It has been called Brazil's answer to St Tropez, a description that is reflected in its prices at least.

Situated 169km (105 miles) east of Rio, Búzios is only a couple of hours by bus, car or even taxi from the city, but is best avoided during the peak season (December to February), when it is uncomfortably overcrowded and overpriced.

Over the centuries, the peninsula's shores have attracted pirates, slave traders and whalers and, more recently, Brigitte Bardot. When the international actress stepped barefoot onto the sands with her Brazilian boyfriend in the 1960s, Búzios – then little more than a fishing village – was projected onto the world's tourist radar. It still retains some of its small-town charm, with most of the accommodation in villas and small, although admittedly increasingly upmarket, *pousadas*.

Beaches

All of Búzios' 25 or so beaches are accessible on a day trip – either by car, taxi, beach buggy or trolley bus. Generally, those in the south are prettier, but more inaccessible, while those on the Atlantic (eastern coast) are cooler and windier. Ferradura is a mushroom-shaped cove, with good snorkelling and diving and access to the lovely Ponta da Lagoinha. Tartaruga is characterised by interesting rock pools and reefs, while the sands of João Fernandes Beach are home to many lively bars. Geribá is a long, open expanse with lots of water sports and surfing, and is popular with the younger generation. Manguinhos is a centre for windsurfing, where boats leave for Isla Feia (Ugly Island), another great diving spot.

Community spirit

There are three communities on the peninsula. Ossos (Bones) on the northern tip has a yacht club and is the least developed; its name comes from the whale skeletons once found on the beach here. Then there is the less attractive Manguinhos. Armação de Búzios has the best facilities for tourists in terms of restaurants, shops, *pousadas* and banks. Here, locals and tourists wander the pedestrian sand streets around Rua das Pedras, shopping in the chic boutiques and art galleries and eating locally caught lobster and giant squid and international food ranging from Thai to Moroccan in the sophisticated restaurants.

On the water

Boat tours – choose from large schooners, small fishing boats and glass-bottomed catamarans – leave from Armação Beach. Trips last anything from an hour to a full day and tickets can be bought at agencies in Rua das Pedras. Specialist boats for fishing, diving and water sports can be hired throughout the peninsula, which has no less than four sailing clubs.

Walks

Trails lead through the peninsula's lush interior, suitable for walking and mountain biking. The Atlantic forest of **Emerências Reserve** is home to exotic plants and the endangered, though easily spotted, golden tamarin monkey. Ecological walks through the reserve leave several times a week from Caravelas Beach, led by **IEBMA** (*Instituto Ecológico Búzios Mata Atlântica, Estrada Velha de Búzios Km 5. Tel: (22) 2623 2200*). **Tauá Reserve** (*www.reservataua.com.br. Open: 8am–6pm. Free admission*) covers a geologically important area full of butterflies, birds and orchids; guided tours can be booked in advance with IEBMA, or just turn up and explore either reserve on your own.

A scenic cove in Búzios

Costa Verde

'Oh God, if there were a paradise on Earth, it wouldn't be far from here.' *(Explorer Amerigo Vespucci).*

The 'Green Coast', with its tropical mountains falling into the clear green sea, is aptly named. Snaking Highway BR-101 begins just west of central Rio, and as it heads south develops into one of the most spectacular coastal drives in the world. On the right the mountains are swathed in dense green rainforest, to the left the blue water stretches to the horizon, studded with empty, white-sand beaches, islands and the occasional palm tree.

Only a tiny 5 per cent of the original 'Mata Atlântica' forest remains here and it is vulnerable to exploitation, but nevertheless the jungle consumes all in

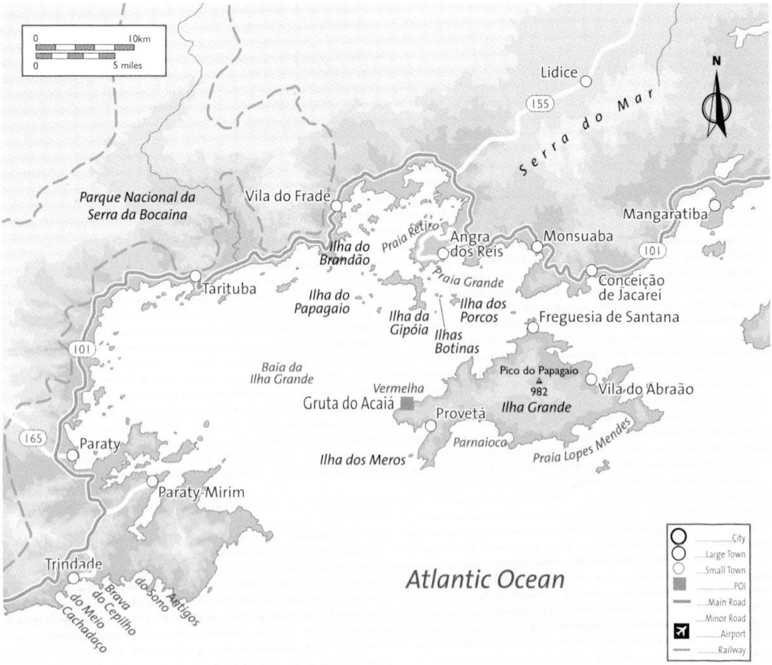

The 'green coast' south of Rio

its path, its mounds of green appearing like some prehistoric emerald monster. This is a coast rich in a history tied to both the forest and the sea, a history heavy with pirates, prisons, gold and rum. There are fishing settlements with traditional Indian names where indigenous people still live, yet heavy industry too, and there are national parks, such as Parque Nacional da Serra da Bocaína.

Take to the water by boat to reach beaches and islands, or even dive underneath it to swim amongst colourful fish and explore shipwrecks from the last five centuries – casualties of battles between the colonists, pirates and Indians, or latterly the wild storms that sometimes hit the coast.

Getting there

Allow four hours to get to Paraty from Rio, which can be done by bus, car or even boat. The whole coast is Rio's (and São Paulo's) playground and is best avoided at weekends and from December to January, if possible. During these times, not only are prices higher and the best accommodation booked up, but these intimate, relaxing spots become overrun by tourists and lose some of their appeal.

Boat trips from Angra lead to hidden coves

ANGRA DOS REIS (COVE OF THE KINGS)

As the fathers of European colonialism, the Portuguese controlled parts of Africa and had claimed lands on the Atlantic coast of modern-day Brazil long before the idea occurred to the British or the French. On 'Kings' Day' 1502, they came across this paradisiacal inlet south of Rio, and named it accordingly. For hundreds of years it was a focal point for piracy and disorder, but today it is a peaceful gateway to the clear waterways and luscious island beaches that surround it.

Angra

The port city of Angra, as it is known, is an odd mixture of tourism and industry. Hulking oil platforms loom over the port, and 20km (12½ miles) down the coast are both of Brazil's nuclear power plants. The port itself is a hub for tankers, trawlers and smaller fishing boats, but also for tourists sailing to Ilha Grande (*see p50*) and the hundreds of other islands in the bay that spread out from here southwest to Paraty. Ferries to Ilha Grande leave from the pier of Cais Santa Luiza (*Avenida Reis Magos. Departure: Mon–Fri 3.30pm, Sat & Sun 1.30pm. Duration: 1½ hours*), and from here visitors can also negotiate other transfers and fishing trips with local operators.

Beaches and resorts

Little more than 2km (1¼ miles) from the port, travelling southwest along the coast road, is Praia Grande, a pleasant sandy beach. North of the city, on the other side of the peninsula, is Praia Retiro, less visited but home to some charming *pousadas* (intimate hotels).

Serra do Mar

Visitors arriving from Rio may be tempted to head straight to the beaches, but a short diversion inland is well worthwhile. Rising up behind Angra is the thickly forested Serra do Mar (Mountain Range of the Sea). Thanks to the steep escarpments, this remains one of the few parts of Brazil's Mata Atlântica (Atlantic Rainforest) that have not been felled. The best way to see it is by rail; during the week, industrial freight is hauled to steel plants inland, but at weekends tourist trains travel the 40km (25 miles) over the mountains to Lidíce with many scenic stops along the way at waterfalls, rivers and viewpoints. *Train tickets from Montmar Turismo. Rua do Comércio 11, Angra dos Reis. Tel: (24) 365 1705. Departure: Sat & Sun 10.30am, returning 4.30pm.*

Underwater

Below the waves, the sea off Angra is a living haven of natural wonders, and a graveyard for many of the piratical corsairs who did battle here. With such clear waters, it is possible to see a great deal with just a snorkel and a pair of flippers, particularly around Ilha dos Porcos and Ilhas Botinas (3km/2 miles south of Angra's port), where huge and colourful schools of fish dart back and forth. For those wishing to venture further afield and deeper, sunken treasure awaits (*see 'Sunken treasure', pp54–5*).

The clear waters give up their treasures

ILHA GRANDE

This lush green island of palm trees, mangroves, waterfalls and white-sand beaches is only 160km (100 miles) south of Rio. Many of the 100 or so beaches are empty stretches of sand, and the only real settlement, Vila do Abraão, is just a laid-back strip of low-lying, prettily coloured buildings. The special environment of the island is protected and cars are forbidden, making it a wonderfully relaxing spot that feels like an undiscovered 'Treasure Island'.

INSIDER INFORMATION

Ilha Grande is reached by a 90-minute boat trip from either Angra dos Reis or Mangaratiba, with normally only one sailing a day from each port. Boat schedules mean that a minimum two-night stay is needed to make a trip worthwhile. The more upmarket hotels are really mini resorts with their own beaches, and they tend to overcharge for everything from drinks to boat transport. There are no banks and most places, even hotels, don't accept credit cards, so bring enough cash for the duration.

History: Forces of evil

The reason why this island is so wonderfully undeveloped is a dark one. Even its early history as a leper colony and a slave trading port is overshadowed by what some Brazilians call the 'forces of evil'. Recent dictatorships used Ilha Grande as a dumping ground for political prisoners and some of the country's most dangerous criminals. These two disparate forces combined to form the

The pristine sands of Lopes Mendes

Commando Vermelho (Red Command) in 1969, which fought the country's dictatorship, and then went on to dominate the country's drug trafficking. The island was only opened to tourists in 1994 when the high-security prison closed.

Boats

Most boat trips leave from Abraão pier; information and tickets are available in the village. One of the most popular trips is the return ride to the beautiful, 3-km (2-mile) long Lopes Mendes, which some say is one of the best beaches in the world. The 50-minute boat ride only takes passengers as far as Pouso pier, from where it is a one-hour walk to the beach. Instead, consider making the spectacular three-hour walk there and taking the boat back.

Alternatively, sail by schooner to Freguesia de Santana, visiting the pretty church of the same name dating from 1796 and stopping off at snorkelling spots along the way, such as the appropriately named Lagoa Azul (Blue Lagoon), full of brightly coloured fish.

Other diving trips are also available, but if you prefer to do your own thing and enjoy the views above water, kayaking in the calm waters of the bay will be a memorable experience.

Hikes and bikes

Hiking through the Atlantic forest to beaches and waterfalls is a real pleasure, especially from May to July when the weather is cooler and there is less rain.

Ilha Grande's Blue Lagoon

Although the many trails are well marked (one circles the whole island and takes a week), a good guide can point out the plants and wildlife. The 982-m (3,222-ft) Pico do Papagaio is a challenging three-hour climb up to the summit surrounded by monkey- and bird-filled jungle, with sweeping views.

If you prefer a bit of pedal power to help you cover more ground, you'll find bikes for hire in the town.

Relaxation

Week-long retreats, combining yoga and massage with hiking, surfing and kayaking, are both challenging and restorative, but come at a price (*www.bodysouladventures.com*).

PARATY

This lovely little colonial town with its family-run pousadas may be full of tourists wandering the cobbled streets in the evening, but during the day most visitors are on day trips and it is relatively quiet. Although ideally situated halfway between the cities of São Paulo and Rio de Janeiro, Paraty, like Ilha Grande, has been incredibly preserved thanks to the relative inaccessibility of both the town and its beaches. Its beautiful deep bay of turquoise water dotted with green islands is best explored by boat.

History: Golden days

Almost 500 years ago, Paraty was exporting endless gallons of *cachaça* to the rest of the country.

The cobbled colonial streets of Paraty

INSIDER INFORMATION

Watch out for 'ecological tours' in Paraty. Agencies proclaim their green credentials on glossy brochures advertising speedboat trips and coach tours with little regard for the environment. **Paraty Adventure** (*Tel: (24) 3371 6135. www.paratyadventure.com*) advertises on recycled paper, is run by locals, and offers small tours to beaches and traditional communities, combining boat trips with walking trails and horse-riding options.

In the early 1800s, gold, diamonds and emeralds were being carried to its port from the interior on the backs of slaves and donkeys, from where they were shipped to Portugal's king. Paraty became one of the wealthiest cities in Brazil and its exquisite houses and churches date from this time, but when an alternative mule trail was built direct to Rio, the town was largely forgotten. It rose again with the coffee boom in the mid-19th century, when mules from the hills brought down beans bound for Europe, and returned with imported porcelain, fabrics and even pianos for the barons.

To the beach

Every day around noon, former fishing and whaling vessels and large purpose-built schooners leave from Paraty's pier loaded with tourists. Either buy a ticket beforehand with a tour agency, bargain with the boatmen on the day, or charter your own. All trips visit a number of beaches, with the chance to swim or snorkel. Faster boats will get you to the more remote beaches, while larger vessels tend to offer more of a 'booze cruise' with lunch, drinks and onboard music. Trindade is a one-time fishing village 25km ($15^1/_2$ miles) from Paraty, reached by bus or taxi, with a number of lovely, popular beaches.

Into the interior

The nomadic Guaianá Indians cut many trails through the dense Atlantic Rainforest, which were later used by the conquerors to transport sugar, gold and coffee. The lush interior is a beautiful region of waterfalls, partly covered by Parque Nacional da Serra da Bocaina, (Serra da Bocaina National Park) where historic farms and the original Caminho do Ouro (Gold Trail) can be visited by tourists, on foot, horse, jeep or even mountain bike. Ask at **Paraty Adventure** (*see opposite*) for more information.

FLIP

A co-founder of the Bloomsbury publishing empire, Liz Calder, who owns a house in Paraty, only set up the Festa Literária Internacional de Parati (Paraty International Literary Festival, *www.flip.org.br*) in 2004, but each July since then has seen it attract an increasing number of luminaries from around the world. Locals delight in seeing the likes of Salman Rushdie eating a giant pasty on the bridge, and there are music performances, and workshops for children.

Fishing and tour boats line Paraty's dock

Excursion: Sunken treasure

Diving in the waters of the Costa Verde, the temptation is to suspend belief and imagine that life above the waves does not exist. Under the water is a completely different world, and there is nowhere better to experience it than here, where breathtakingly clear waters reveal countless schools of tropical fish, alive with colour and movement. Well-preserved wrecks, dating back years, decades and centuries have become shelters for sea life and exciting visual treats for the diver.

Dive excursions can be arranged from Angra dos Reis, Ilha Grande or Paraty. All have reputable dive clubs, though Paraty is quite a distance from the best wreck diving sites.

Cave and night dives

The **Gruta do Acaiá** is a shallow cave where sunlight makes the sea and rock sparkle. For those who want to go deeper, the **Parcel do Coronel** drops

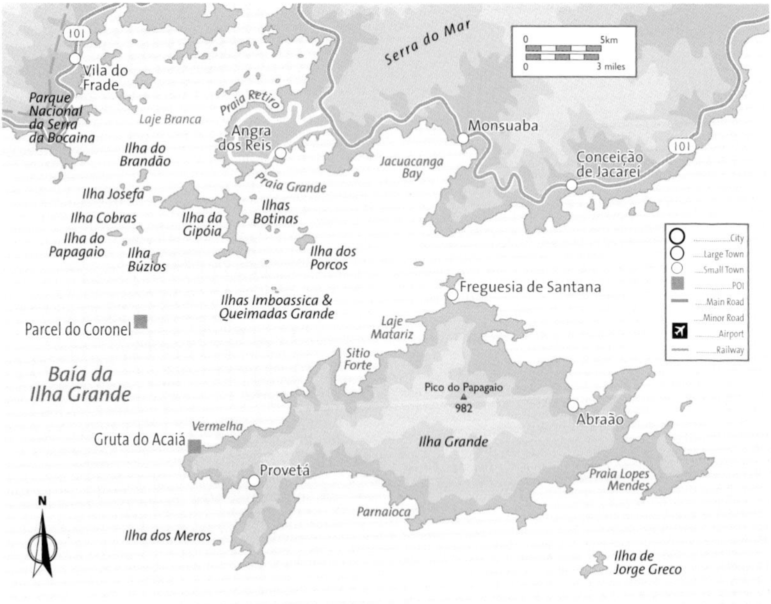

Fish fill the crystal-clear waters

as deep as 25m (82ft). After dark, experienced divers can kit up with torches for a night dive in **Laje Branca**.

Fishing

The waters off **Ilha dos Meros** are a perfect spot for underwater spear fishing, for those with a hunger to catch their own lunch. Chances are your captain will be happy to steer you to a beach restaurant to have it grilled and served up with a *caipirinha*.

Sea life

The islands of **Brandão**, **Josefa** and **Papagaio** are prime sites to spot sea sponges, coral and brightly coloured fish, as are **Imboassica** and **Queimadas Grande**. The waters off the **Ilhas Botinas** and **Ilha dos Porcos** are so abundant in fish and so clear that you can see enormous schools, even from a boat. And near the islands of **Búzios** and **Cobras**, it is possible to coast through fascinating *parcéis* (rock channels) 4–12m (13–40ft) deep.

For those with little experience, a trip to **Ilhas Botinas** is a good choice. These two islets offer shallow water, with excellent visibility and plenty of interesting fish.

Wreck dives

There are 16 wrecks currently being investigated at the bottom of Angra's bay, one of the highest concentrations anywhere in the world. At Parnaioca, the ***Vapor Japurá*** went down in 1860. Six years later, the ***Califórnia*** went down at Vermelha. In 1906, the ***Encouraçado Aquidabã*** was sunk in Jacuacanga Bay. More recently (1966), a Panamanian freighter called the ***Pinguino*** sank in Sitio Forte, and it is possible for divers to explore the engine room and cabins. In Laje Matariz, there is the wreck of a helicopter 7m (23ft) below the surface. If the currents are still enough, it can be made out from the surface with just a snorkelling mask. And close to one of the bay's jutting headlands is the ***Bezerra de Menezes***, a steam-driven freighter that sank in 1860.

The south

The south of Brazil is home to the gridlocked tangle of São Paulo, an urban sprawl that is a vertical metaphor for society as a whole. The poorest live in the gutter and the middle classes in low-rise apartment blocks, while the super rich are rarely seen below the 20th floors. São Paulo has more helicopters than anywhere else in the world (more even than Manhattan) and they can be seen all day ferrying businesspeople from their gated mansions to the rooftop helipads of their offices and to lunch appointments.

São Paulo is where Brazil's president, Lula, got his first real job, working in a steel factory before he was 16, and it is where the harsh treatment dished out to the unions drove him into politics and the campaign for a new Brazil. Visitors to São Paulo can enjoy the distractions of its fine cuisine, cultural scene and heady nightlife, but it can be an oppressive city. Unlike Rio, São

Paulo has no beach, so come the weekend those who can afford it take flight to the coast of Santa Catarina and the island of the same name, where there are countless beaches to suit all tastes, from wild surfers' outposts to family-friendly resorts with calm, warm waters.

Further south, on the border with Argentina, are the spectacular cascades of Iguaçu, which dwarf the famous Niagara Falls in both height and width. In the midst of the southern jungle, the town of Foz do Iguaçu is nondescript, but its airport and regular flights from all over Brazil give convenient access to the falls and the beautiful national park that surrounds them.

Ilha Santa Catarina's Praia Galheta

SÃO PAULO: HEDONISTIC CITY

Few places in Brazil are as cosmopolitan as this sprawling megalopolis, where 11 million people live and double that number work. Built and driven by immigration, São Paulo is home to large Italian and Japanese communities, bustling neighbourhood restaurants and an exciting nightlife scene. The city is a creative centre to rival Rio, with high-quality art, film and theatre to the fore, while the international cuisine on offer is some of the best in the world. The district of Cerqueira César, at the north end of Avenida Paulista, is where hard-working locals and tourists alike throng at the weekend with fun in mind.

Culture vultures

Paulistinos (residents of the city) are spoilt for choice when it comes to the arts. The following are some of the highlights.

A bustling local street market

WHEN IN ROME...

In this city, it pays to live by local rules. Over 90 per cent of the country's power is hydroelectric, and, with perennial drought a major problem, power cuts are common in this energy-intensive hub. Office workers who find their PCs down and lights out are usually to be found in street cafés and bars throughout the city. Why not join them? In the morning, the drink of choice is a *cafezinho*, a strong espresso to set you up for the day. After lunch, *guarana* is a speedy drink made from Amazonian fruit, and in the evening, it's on to *caipirinha*, the national cocktail made with limes, sugar and the powerful spirit *cachaça*.

Centro Cultural Banco do Brasil

The centre is a relative newcomer on the cultural scene, though the building, one of the city's first banks, opened over 100 years ago. It hosts films, plays and sometimes exhibitions down in the old vaults. Telephone in advance to arrange guided tours around this fine example of neoclassical architecture.
Rua Álvares Penteado 112. Tel: (11) 3113 3600/3651. Open: Tue–Sun 10am–8pm.

Sala São Paulo

The Sala occupies the grand former hall of a railway station and is home to the State Symphony Orchestra. With an adjustable acoustic ceiling, it is reputed to be one of the best classical music venues in the world.
Praça Júlio Prestes. Tel: (11) 3351 8286 (tours) and 3357 5414 (tickets).

www.salasaopaulo.art.br (Portuguese only).

Teatro Municipal

São Paulo's municipal theatre was designed in the style of the Paris Opera House. The grand building dates from 1911 and is home to two full orchestras and a myriad of other musical and dance outfits. There are free concerts every Wednesday at 12.30pm and free guided tours around the building on Tuesday and Thursday at noon and 1pm. The city's official ballet company, Balé da Cidade (*www.baledacidade.com.br, Portuguese only*), also performs here. *Praça Ramos de Azevedo. Tel: (11) 3222 8698. www.prefeitura.sp.gov.br/theatromunicipal (Portuguese only).*

The high life

This is a city of skyscrapers, from the modernist **Edifício Copan** (*Avenida Iparanga 200*) to the **Prédio do Banespa**, which is a slightly smaller version of the Empire State Building, and offers great views of the city (*Rua João Brícola 24. Tel: (11) 3249 7405. Free guided tours Mon–Fri 10am–5pm*).

The powerhouse of São Paulo

The beautiful game

Pelé entitled his 1977 autobiography *My Life and the Beautiful Game,* and for him and most of his countrymen, the two are inextricably linked. That this particular Brazilian should have coined the now universal phrase is fitting. The unstoppable duo of Pelé striking through the middle, with Garrincha terrorising defences on the right wing, came to represent the golden era of Brazilian football.

The ethos of the Brazilian game has always been 'attack from anywhere'.

A bust of Garrincha at the Botafogo football club

Successive teams have paid almost scant regard to the tactics of the opposition, confident in the belief that whatever happens, however many goals Brazil concedes, the team will score more. Their success lies in their love for the ball, reflected everywhere you go in Brazil.

Unstoppable and everywhere

In Rio, workers queue overnight to hire out five-a-side pitches on Saturday morning, and flood-lit 'beach soccer' pitches are full throughout the night with shift-workers getting their fix of the national obsession. Every day on the beach, countless groups play barefoot 'keepy-uppy' (passing the ball to each other for as long as possible without it landing in the sand or sea). Others take part in the serious and hugely popular sport of 'footvolley', beach volleyball using the head, feet and chest. Rocinha (the biggest *favela* in Rio) proudly boasts one of the best-known champions.

Futsal (derived from *futebol de salão*, 'drawing room football') is an indoor five-a-side version of the game, where the heavy small ball very rarely leaves the ground. Some of Brazil's best players, including Zico,

Celebrating another Brazilian victory

Ronaldo and Ronaldinho, learned their skills playing this game. Oil-rig workers play on small, fenced-in pitches next to the helipad. In the Amazon, pitches are sometimes raised up on stilts, or if not, players just wade through the flood water and play on regardless.

The Brazilians were playing 'button football' almost 30 years before Waddington's invented the ubiquitous table-football game Subbuteo, and nothing gets in the way of their love of the game. The country recently reached the final of the blind football World Cup, where a necessarily silent audience watches sightless competitors play with a ball that contains noisy ball bearings. From the sidelines, coaches shout tactical guidance to midfielders and defenders, but in front of the goal attackers display flamboyant finishing that simply cannot be taught.

The greats

Pelé is of course 'the King', justly revered for his all-round professionalism, skill and goal scoring ability, but in many ways, Garrincha is the people's champion. Born with deformed legs to a poor family in the north of Brazil, he almost single-handedly won the World Cup in 1962 (Pelé was injured). Garrincha had little ambition beyond tormenting defences and having a good time. Eventually his legs gave way, and his love of the good life ended his playing career. In 1982 he died the ignominious death of an alcoholic, while Pelé went on to be Sports Minister and one of the most influential figures in world football. The game is still one of the only outlets for Brazil's poor to escape to wealth and glory, but *joga bonito* (playing beautifully) remains as important as winning.

FLORIANÓPOLIS AND SANTA CATARINA

Florianópolis is the capital of Santa Catarina, one of Brazil's wealthier states, which attracts many domestic and international holidaymakers. The city sits partly on the mainland and partly on the west coast of the island of Santa Catarina. Most visitors whiz across the new bridge heading for the busy resorts of the northwest with their sheltered, warm waters, or the wild, unpopulated south of the island, where cold, powerful currents and spectacular breakers are perfect for hardy surfers.

Praia Mole on Ilha Santa Catarina

Ilha Santa Catarina

One of the most popular family resorts on Floripa (as the island is sometimes known) is Praia da Daniela, 3km (2 miles) of white sands on a headland 20km (12½ miles) north of the city. Jurerê Internacional is a larger, family-friendly resort with shops, bars and restaurants, less than 5km (3 miles) up along the coast from Daniela. Between the two is a short stretch of rocky coastline guarded by the cannons of the Fortaleza de São José (1741) and the peaceful Praia de Forte.

Beauty spots

For those who want to get away from the hubbub, Armação is 8km (5 miles) south of Lagoa da Conceição, the island's central freshwater lake, and is a favourite with surfers thanks to the crashing cold waves. Perhaps the most beautiful beach on the whole island is Lagoinha do Leste, which is a 4-km (2½-mile) hike from the small town of Pântano do Sul, 6km (3¾ miles) south of Armação. Closer to the resorts of the north, Praia Moçambique is a 12-km (7½-mile) stretch of unspoilt beach on the edge of a forest reserve.

Party spots

Praia Brava on the northernmost tip of the island is where young people gather every day to play and people-watch. The water is fairly warm and the high waves are good for surfing. Heading south along the east coast of the island, clothing is optional at Praia Galheta,

The aquamarine waters of Lagoa da Conceição

and between it and the surfer's beach, Praia Mole, there is a gay hang-out. Close to busy east-coast beaches such as Mole and Joaquina, the lakeside circuit is full of restaurants and bars that attract diners and partygoers as soon as the sun goes down.

Mainland

Culture

Whilst the island of Santa Catarina has much to offer, the mainland should not be overlooked. Located 125km (77½ miles) south of Florianópolis, past the low-key surfers' beaches around Garopaba, is the picture-postcard seaside town of Laguna with hundreds of buildings dating back to the 17th and 18th centuries. The **Museu Anita Garibaldi** is worth a visit to learn about the 1839 'July Republic' that sprung up here in opposition to the empire (*Praça da República Juliana, Laguna. Tel: (48) 3644 4947*).

Diving

The Bombinhas peninsula, 55km (34 miles) up the coast from Florianópolis, offers probably the best snorkelling and scuba diving in southern Brazil, with clear waters that open up views to a world of magnificent undersea colour. With visibility of up to 25m (82ft), it is no wonder the offshore **Reserva Biológica Marinha do Avoredo** has become so popular. Dives can be arranged with registered excursions only; try **Submarine** (*Tel: (47) 3369 2473*) or **Patadacobra** (*Tel: (47) 3369 2119*).

Excursion: Iguaçu Falls and Parque Nacional do Iguaçu

The Iguaçu waterfalls are one of the most impressive natural wonders in the world, set in a national park that is a UNESCO World Heritage Site. The giant crescent of 275 waterfalls is 2.7km ($1^2/_3$ miles) wide and 82m (269ft) high, nearly two and a half times the width, and 30m (98ft) higher, than glorified Niagara. The waterfalls were a sacred place for the Tupi Guarani Indians who named them Iguaçu, meaning 'great waters'. The spectacular falls sit like a jewel in an exquisite setting of emerald green, coloured with tropical birds, butterflies, rainbows and rare orchids. Enormous clouds of spray water the lush vegetation that hides rare giant otters and anteaters.

A shuttle bus links Macuco, Cataratas and Porto Canoas with its restaurant and shops, and the visitor centre. From the Cataratas stop, a 1.2-km ($^3/_4$-mile) trail zigzags down to the river and a spectacular walkway right up to the aptly named Garganta del Diablo (Devil's Throat).

Parque Nacional do Iguaçu. Tel: (45) 3521 4400. www.cataratasdoiguacu.com.br. Open: 9am–5pm (Apr–Sept); 9am–6pm (Oct–Mar). Admission charge.

Tours

Campo de Desafios offers rafting and climbing trips in the Iguaçu canyon. **Macuco Ecoaventura** arranges boat rides down the river in kayaks or motorboats and guided bike or walking trails of varying lengths through the park. For three nights every month there are magical full-moon tours (contact the national park office, above, for information).

The **Macuco Safári** is by far the most popular trip in the park. Electric cars take passengers through the jungle, while guides give information about the plant and animal life. An optional walking trail leads to the river where lifejackets and plastic bags to protect cameras are handed out. An inflatable boat then bounces off through the rocky canyon at full throttle to beat the ferocious current. Passengers are taken right up to the base of the falls, and then under it as many as three times.

Campo de Desafios. www.campodedesafios.com.br

Macuco Ecoaventura. www.macucoecoaventura.com.br

Macuco Safári. Tel: (45) 523 6475.

www.macucosafari.com.br. Departure: every ten minutes. Duration: 1¾ hours.

Parque Nacional Iguazú Argentina

The Argentinian side of the national park is well worth seeing too; allow a day for each side. Brazil may have the better view, but Argentina boasts more of the falls and offers a much more intimate experience. The trip can easily be done by taxi, but don't forget to take your passport.

From the entrance to this sprawling area of subtropical rainforest, the Tren de la Selva (Jungle Train) takes passengers to the 0.6-km (⅓-mile) long Circuito Superior (Upper Circuit), which provides the best overall view, as well as to the 1.7-km (1-mile) Circuito Inferior (Lower Circuit), offering close-ups of individual cascades and a not-to-be-missed boat ride to Isla San Martín. The final stop is the Garganta del Diablo Station and a walkway to the edge of the 'Devil's Throat'.

Parque Nacional. www.iguazuargentina.com. Open: 7.30am–6.30pm (Oct–Mar); 8am–6pm (Apr–Sept). Admission charge.

The centre

The central state of Minas Gerais (General Mines) is where the Portuguese discovered the vast hoards of gold, diamonds and gems that propped up their empire for centuries. Rich colonial towns grew up around these discoveries, with imposing churches and grand mansions built by the gold barons who got rich quick. Wealthy merchants and poor miners stayed in towns like Ouro Preto, Diamantina and Tiradentes until the mines dried up.

To the west of this region, bordering Paraguay and Bolivia, is the Pantanal, a land rich in plant and animal life that floods and dries with the seasonal rains. The area around the Pantanal was known by the Portuguese simply as Mato Grosso (Thick Forest), and for biodiversity it rivals the Amazon. In terms of visible wildlife, it is even more impressive, with mammals such as monkeys, jaguars, wolves and deer, reptiles like the anaconda, and hundreds of bird species, large and small.

With almost no subsequent investment after the end of the mining era, and little impetus to change, many of the colonial towns of the Minas

The golden churches of Minas Gerais speak of Brazil's past wealth

Gerais remain much as they were. The evocative, scenic Estrada Real (Royal Road), along which the wealth was taken to the coast on the backs of donkeys and slaves, links these towns together. To follow this trail is to step back in time, past gushing waterfalls, rocky peaks and remote hillside settlements.

The natural wonders of the Pantanal area have also largely been protected over the centuries, because the floods have made large-scale cultivation and settlement almost impossible. However, the area's delicate balance is now threatened by 'improvement schemes' that aim to create year-round navigable waterways by draining some parts and permanently flooding others. By travelling to this wilderness with a responsible tour operator, visitors can contribute to an alternative local economy based on showcasing rather than destroying this fragile ecosystem.

OURO PRETO

Ouro Preto is a gold-rush town that was stranded in time when the gold ran out. But before that happened, wily merchants, the Church and the Portuguese Crown got rich off the back of the miners who toiled below ground. A wonderful legacy was left behind, artistically and architecturally, which survives to this day, albeit a little ragged at the edges. The best way to explore is on foot, but be prepared for some steep climbs on cobbled streets.

Historic houses

Casa dos Contos

The old gold counting house is a well-preserved museum documenting the gold-rush days.

Rua São José. Tel: (31) 3551 1444. Open: Tue–Sat 12.30–5pm, Sun 9am–3pm. Admission charge.

Museu da Inconfidência

Before they were taken to the gallows or exiled to Africa, the leaders of Brazil's first rebellion against the monarchy were kept in Ouro Preto's city gaol. This is now the **Museu da Inconfidência**, named after the anti-royalist movement, and it houses the exhumed remains of 12 of those executed, including their leader Tiradentes (Tooth Puller).

Praça Tiradentes 139. Tel: (31) 3551 1121. Open: Tue–Sun noon–5.30pm. Admission charge.

Museu de Mineralogia

The history of this area is tied in with the precious gems that made it rich, and there are some stunning pieces on show in the old governor's mansion, now the **Museu de Mineralogia**. Inside is one of Aleijadinho's fountains.

Nossa Senhora do Carmo overlooks the town

Praça Tiradentes 20. Tel: (31) 3559 1597. Open: Tue–Sun noon–5pm.

Teatro Municipal Casa da Ópera
Brazil's oldest operational theatre and opera house is in Ouro Preto. Visitors can walk around the theatre during the day or take in a show in the evening.
Rua Brig. Musqueira. Tel: (31) 3559 3224. Visits: noon–5.30pm.

Religious riches

UNESCO recognised the historic importance of the town when it was made a World Heritage Site in 1980. Many of the churches were designed or contain important sculptures by the masterful Aleijadinho (*see 'Colonial towns', pp70–71*), while paintings by the equally skilled Mestre Ataíde, born in nearby Mariana, adorn the walls.

Igreja de Nossa Senhora do Carmo
Built in 1766, this church watches over the town from its vantage point above. The church contains some of Aleijadinho's last sculptures and a sacristy painting by Ataíde. Next door, the monks' quarters are home to the **Museu do Oratório**, which displays examples of religious art from the colonial days to the present. The museum's name comes from the altars and prayer cabinets housing carved saints, of which there are over 150 examples on display.
Rua Brig. Musqueira. www.oratorio.com.br. Church open: Tue–Sat noon–4.45pm, Sun 10–11am & 1–4.30pm. Museum open: 9.30am–5.30pm. Admission charge.

Igreja de São Francisco de Assis
The rococo-style Church of St Francis of Assisi is one of the town's most impressive buildings and was built in 1776. Aleijadinho designed the whole church, sculpted the monumental doorway from soft soapstone, figures to decorate the pulpit, the altar and intricate panelling around the chapel. The fanciful ceiling, painted by Ataíde, cleverly distorts perspective to make the cherubim and angels appear even more heavenly.
Largo de Coimbra. Open: Tue–Sun 8.30–11.50am & 1.30–5pm. Admission charge.

Ouro Preto's steep streets demand fitness

Colonial towns

Throughout the region around Ouro Preto, mineral wealth meant that colonial masterpieces were created by architect Aleijadinho (*see box*), painter Mestre Ataíde and the countless and nameless African slaves who toiled and died for the Church and Crown. Once wealthy towns such as Congonhas and Tiradentes, and further afield Diamantina, demonstrate the creative power of this triumvirate. Beautiful as this legacy is, there must also be sadness that Brazil's wealth was not put to better use.

Congonhas

Unlike Ouro Preto, this mining town is not generally well preserved, but it is home to Aleijadinho's *Prophets*, an outstanding collection of 12 Old-Testament sculptures that adorn the steps of the **Basilica de Bom Jesus de Matossinhos** (1761). In the garden courtyard of the church are six chapels with scores of life-size biblical depictions, sculpted to serve as important tools for an evangelising church in a largely illiterate age.

500kg (1,100lbs) of gold adorn the interior of the church at Tiradentes

Diamantina

Built on the back of diamond finds in the 18th century, this town, like Ouro Preto, is a World Heritage Site. It is a five-hour bus journey north from the state capital Belo Horizonte, and few visitors make the journey. However, with colonial houses locked in time, grand churches and scenic hikes on offer, more and more are making the journey (*see 'Head for the hills', pp72–3*).

Mariana

Just 15km (9 1/3 miles) to the east of Ouro Preto, Mariana, the original state capital, is home to the monumental **Catedral Basilica da Sé**, an opulent religious showcase with a dozen gilded altars, crystal chandeliers and a 300-year-old organ with 1,000 pipes. The term 'jaw-dropping' is no exaggeration here,

One of 12 prophets around the Basilica in Congonhas

particularly during recitals.
Praça Cláudio Manoel.
Open: Tue–Sun 7am–6pm.
Recitals: Fri 11am, Sun 12.15pm.
Admission charge.

ALEIJADINHO (THE LITTLE CRIPPLE)

In 1730, Antônio Francisco Lisboa was born in Ouro Preto. His mother was his father's slave, but this was not the taint in Brazil that it was in North America at the time. He was nicknamed 'Aleijadinho' because he contracted a debilitating disease (thought to be leprosy or syphilis) through which he lost his fingers and toes, as well as the use of his limbs. He developed his own style of playful baroque architecture and sculpture (mostly self-taught) and, despite his illness, went on to create several masterpieces, collaborating with the painter Mestre Ataíde, who was born and is buried in Mariana. Like his friend, Ataíde was mixed race and painted his angels with *mulatto* (black and white mixed race) features.

Tiradentes (Tooth Puller)

Named after the amateur dentist who led Brazil's first (doomed) rebellion against the empire, this is a pretty hillside town, largely forgotten after the 18th-century mining boom. Though its church, **Matriz de Santo António**, is grand enough (close to 500kg/1,100lbs of gold were used to decorate the interior), there is much more here to admire. Artisans sell fine arts and crafts, such as colourful clay pots and pans, and jewellery, candelabras and vases made of silver.

There is a bohemian feel to this peaceful town, which comes alive in January with its film festival, in June when Harley-Davidson motorbike enthusiasts hit town, and in August for its International Culture and Cuisine fair.

Tour: Head for the hills

The Portuguese were the most fearless explorers in the 'old world', and the bandeirantes *of São Paulo (then a village) were the shock troops of the Crown, driving deep into Brazil's interior in search of gold, diamonds and slaves. In Minas Gerais, just lying on the riverbanks, they found chunks of ouro preto ('black gold', named after the coating of iron oxide that had formed on the precious metal). It was carried by slaves and donkeys through the mountains to coastal Paraty, and then along to Rio.*

The route to the coast was named the Estrada Real (Royal Road) and was the rich vein through which Portugal drew out the lifeblood of this virgin land.

Leave early from the state capital of Belo Horizonte to make the most of the scenery on the 290-km (180-mile) road to Diamantina. If you don't wish to drive, buses leave at 5.30am, 9am and 11.30am.

1 Diamantina

The town grew up around nearby diamond mines in the 18th century, and prompted the northern 'Diamond Route' extension of the Estrada Real.
From Diamantina, the trail heads south, through picturesque valleys with free-flowing rivers.

2 São Gonçalo do Rio das Pedras

This old mining village, 36km (22 miles) south of Diamantina, is a pleasant stop with nearby waterfalls that are perfect for a dip.

Much of the overgrown route south to Mariana is currently being restored and reconstructed. Check with the Instituto Estrada Real (www.estradareal.org.br) for updates on completed sections. After Serro, 20km (12½ miles) from São Gonçalo, the trail doglegs to the west before reaching Conceição do Mato Dentro. This section of the route is 77km (48 miles), though the road (MG 010) connecting the two is an option for those with limited time.

3 Conceição do Mato Dentro

Just 6km (3¾ miles) from this small town are the rock carvings of Salão de Pedra and Colina da Paz.
From here it is just over 35km (21¾ miles) south to the hillside town of Morro do Pilar.

4 Parque Nacional da Serra do Cipó

Close to Morro do Pilar is this rarely visited wilderness. Join a tour in the town for hiking or 4WD journeys along the mountain trails.

Travelling south again from Pilar, it is 75km ($46^{1}/_{2}$ miles) to Bom Jesus do Amparo and a further 25km ($15^{1}/_{2}$ miles) to Cocais. From Cocais it is 80km (50 miles) to Mariana.

5 Mariana

After some time in Mariana (*see 'Colonial towns', pp70–71*), you can choose to hike or drive the stretch from Mariana to Ouro Preto, or catch the 1940s steam train, the **Trem da Vale**, which offers a relaxing way to see the countryside.

6 Ouro Preto

From Ouro Preto visitors can choose to follow the 'old route' down to Paraty, or the 'new route', the trail that was carved through the jungle from Ouro Preto direct to Rio in the early 1800s. Hike, bike or ride the trail itself, or hop from place to place by road or rail.

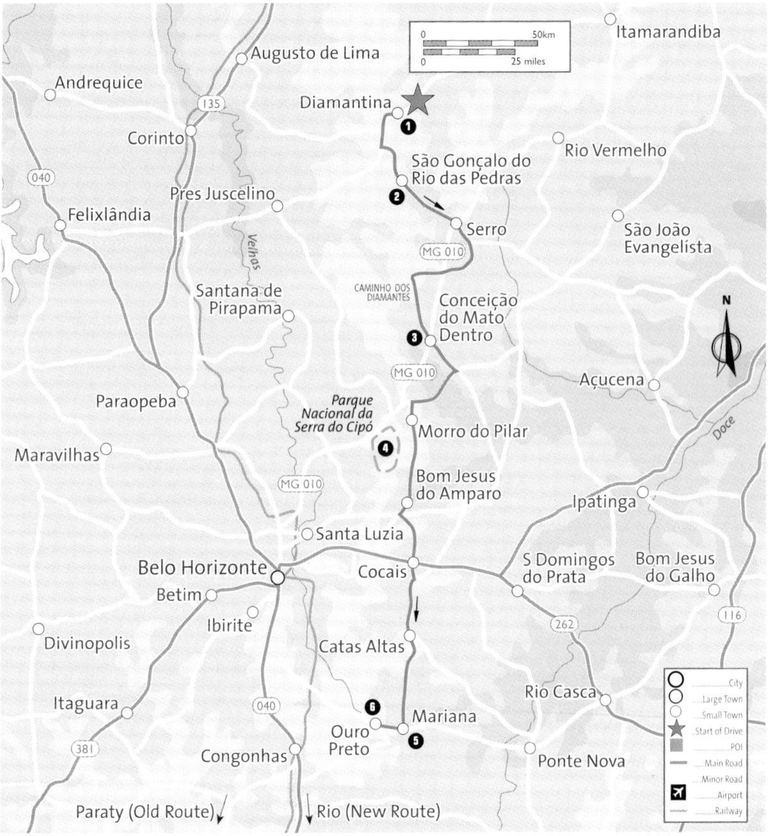

THE PANTANAL

Spreading into Paraguay and Bolivia, the Pantanal is the largest freshwater wetland in the world; the Brazilian share alone is almost the size of England. Literally translated as 'swamp', it is in fact a giant, seasonally flooded plain, which early explorers believed was an inland sea. The whole region forms a natural sanctuary, home to the largest concentration of visible wildlife in South America. Film crews have long known that while the Amazon gets most of the attention, the Pantanal is a much better place to see birds and animals. This is largely thanks to its wide-open savanna and meadows which, unlike the dense rainforest, offer few hiding places for the wild inhabitants.

Wildlife

The Pantanal teems with creatures, many of them seemingly larger than life; it has insects the size of birds, birds as big as children and rodents as large as pigs. The magnificent metre-high jabiru, sporting a black hood and a scarlet collar, is the biggest stork in the world and a fitting symbol of the region. The beautiful, bright blue hyacinth macaw – a giant parrot that is now endangered – reaches the same enormous proportions. Birdwatchers

A caiman tries to sneak up on a jabiru

are in heaven here, with over 700 species, including tiger herons, buff-necked ibis and savanna hawks, the largest variety on the planet. Those who love to fish go wide-eyed over the 200 species that share the waters with piranha and anacondas. Playful howler monkeys drop fruit on visitors' heads and comical families of capybara (a kind of giant guinea pig) can be seen sauntering along the riverside in single file. Sightings of the exquisite jaguar prove more elusive.

No Man's Land?

There may be as many as 30 million caiman in the swampy waters, but only 200,000 people live in this frontier region sometimes known as Tierra de Ningeuem (No Man's Land). Both the indigenous communities with their traditional rituals and the southern cowboys lend it a distinct culture. By day, visitors can sip *tereré* (local iced tea) and fall into the swing of this laid-back region by relaxing by the pool or in a hammock, and at night take part in traditional barbecues under the huge skies that are often set alight by the sinking sun. Don't expect a huge variety of food, but some interesting local specialities, such as sun-dried beef and piranha soup.

A fragile future

Since the late 1980s, the Pantanal's future has been threatened by a newly proposed 'hidrovia', an aquatic motorway which will allow ocean-going river navigation through five landlocked countries, regardless of the season. The dredging of the Paraguay and Parana rivers to achieve this could destroy this vulnerable ecosystem and effectively turn it into a desert.

Additionally, despite attempts to crack down on illegal fishing, hunting, logging and mining in the region, these activities all continue. A host of animals, from parrots and macaws to panthers and caiman, are trafficked illegally for sale as pets.

Uncontrolled tourism is yet another of the Damocles' Swords hanging over this area of worldwide importance. Visitors can play their part by checking the green credentials of hotels and tour agencies.

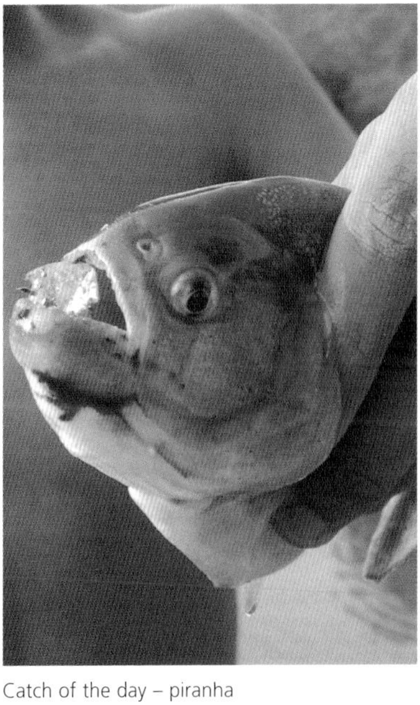

Catch of the day – piranha

Driving a herd in the Pantanal

GETTING TO THE PANTANAL

In the centre of South America, in the west of Brazil, the Pantanal sprawls over the two states of Mato Grosso and Mato Grosso do Sul. Their respective capitals, Cuiabá in the northern part of the Pantanal and Campo Grande in the south, and to a lesser extent the city of Corumbá, are the gateways to this wildlife-spotting region. All three have airports, with daily connections to Brazil's other cities, as well as daily bus links. While all three have good tourist infrastructure, none are destinations in their own rights, merely jumping-off points for this remote area. Those managing to arrive early enough in the morning can get to the Pantanal before nightfall and avoid having to spend a night in the city (travelling in the dark is not safe because of the condition of roads).

Getting organised

The vast majority of visitors will see the Pantanal as part of an organised tour, making arrangements with one of the agencies in the three gateway cities and arriving by bus, boat or even plane. It is also possible to book directly with an accommodation provider. Tours tend to take place at dawn and dusk when wildlife-spotting is at its best, travelling in open-top jeep, by foot, or even by canoe or horse. Night-time safaris are also on offer, in which torches seek out the shining pairs of lights of animals' eyes.

Going it alone

Although it is possible to travel independently with a four-wheel-drive car or even a bicycle, staying at accommodation along the way, it is not as straightforward as you might imagine. The only road through the Pantanal is 150km (93 miles) of raised dirt track known as the Transpantaneira. It runs from Poconé (100km/62 miles southwest of Cuiabá) down to Porto Joffre, there are practically no facilities along the way, and travel after dark is dangerous.

Being practical

The dry season (October–March) is the best time to visit the Pantanal; during the wet season (November–April) when the rivers burst their banks, the whole area is covered in water and transport is only possible by boat, although animals can be spotted taking refuge on *cordilheiras* that form high islands. You need to stay at least two nights on a visit as it takes at least half a day to even arrive; to fully experience the Pantanal, four days is the minimum.

Shops and banks are practically non-existent, so bring all the cash and toiletries you need and maybe even snacks and favourite drinks. Insect repellent, sunscreen, a hat, long sleeves and trousers are a must to protect against the fierce sun and ferocious insects. Binoculars are a really good idea, and can greatly enhance the experience.

Sleeping easy

Accommodation in the Pantanal comes in four guises: *fazendas* (like ranches, probably the most popular option), *pousadas* (small hotels), *pesqueiros* (fishing lodges, normally with rods and boats to hire) and *botels* (expensive, floating hotels). Prices for all reflect the fact that meals, local transport and tours are usually included.

Access to the Pantanal is difficult at the best of times

Bahia

Bahia is altogether a different country from the south; it is hotter, more African, and very much in a different time zone. This is where workers from the powerhouses of São Paulo and Rio de Janeiro come to relax, revelling in the long white-sand beaches with year-round sunshine and a relaxed way of life that is almost Caribbean.

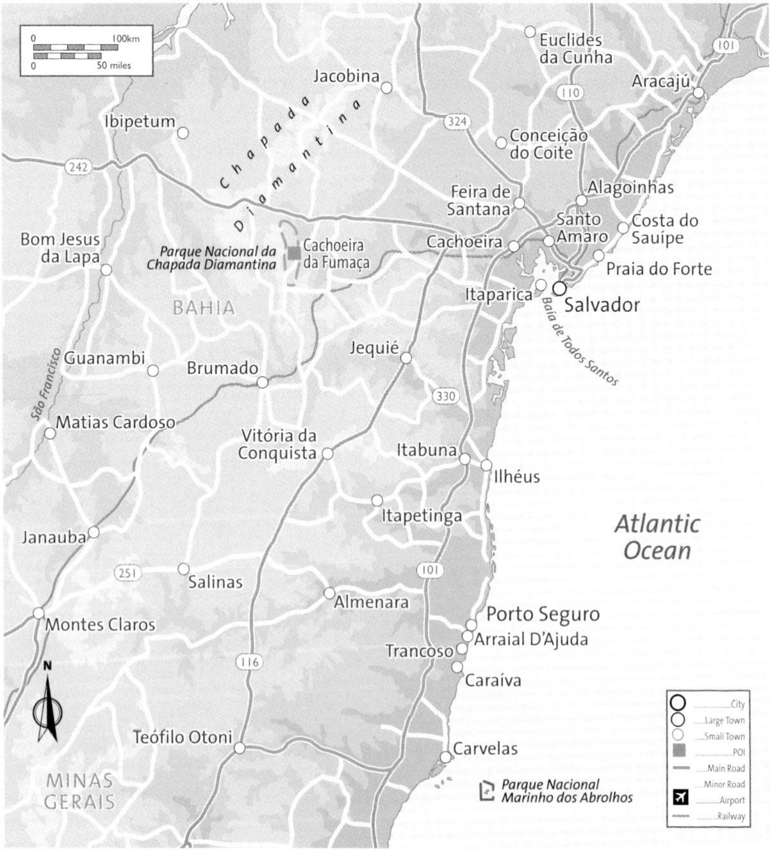

This state is the size of France, with a 1,200-km (746-mile) coastline that is practically one long beach, with small fishing villages, places to party and purpose-built family resorts. Off the coast are a number of laid-back islands, and sanctuaries that protect wildlife such as turtles and whales. In the interior, the Parque Nacional da Chapada Diamantina offers the chance to really get away from it all.

History

In many ways, Salvador *is* Bahia, and Brazilians often use the words interchangeably. Until 1763 Salvador was the capital not only of Brazil but also of the entire Portuguese empire in the Americas. The city was also the Americas' largest port until the 18th century, its wealth fed by the slave trade and the great arc of fertile land known as the Recôncavo that in many ways is the cradle of Brazilian civilisation.

Bahia is also the birthplace of Brazilian popular music. The rich fusion of African, Indian and Brazilian influences has produced some of the world's most exciting music. The Brazilian musical giants Gilberto Gil and Caetano Veloso hail from here, and in the 1960s musicians Janis Joplin and Jimmy Cliff came to stay. Although the popularity of lambada in the 1980s may have waned, tropicalismo, afoxé and axé are still the life blood of music throughout the country, and it all comes to a head with the explosion of vitality, sensuality and music that is Carnaval.

Pleasure vessels wait to whiz passengers around the Bay of All Saints

PORTO SEGURO AND SURROUNDS

The coast around Porto Seguro (which means 'safe port') was where Pedro Cabral and the first Portuguese fleet landed in Brazil in 1500. Today Porto Seguro's airport is where thousands of Brazilian and international tourists land to set off for nearby beaches. It is possible to walk along the sand for kilometres, swimming in clear pools created by the nearby reefs and taking rides on horseback or in fishing boats.

Porto Seguro

The compact historical centre, with two of Brazil's oldest churches and a city museum, sits on a small bluff in the *cidade alta* (upper city). The Portuguese possession of Brazil is marked by a marble monument erected in 1503. The local Pataxó Indians have been largely displaced, but it is possible to buy their crafts all along the coast.

In *cidade baixa* (lower city), the main attraction is Passarela do Álcool (Alcohol Street) and its surrounding roads, lined

The hippy village of Arraial d'Ajuda

The cliffs of Trancoso give way to deserted beaches

with lively bars that stay open all night, serving *capete*, the local cocktail of vodka, milk and cinnamon. Lambada was born in the 1980s in the *barracas* (beach bars) north of town, which now blast out axé and forró. There is a string of beaches here, such as Praia Curuípe with its coral pools, the always-crowded Taperapuã and quieter Itacimirim.

Arraial d'Ajuda

This old Jesuit village just 4km (2½ miles) south of Porto Seguro is reached by a ten-minute ferry ride from the city. Arraial d'Ajuda was discovered by hippies some time ago and has developed very rapidly into a commercial, often crowded, resort.

Trancoso

Trancoso, 25km (15½ miles) south of Porto Seguro, is much more recognisable as a former Jesuit settlement than Arraial d'Ajuda. The lovely grassy church square sits on top of a bluff where horses and dogs roam freely and mango and jacaranda trees surround the delightful multicoloured cottages. The calm has only partly been disturbed by increasing numbers of Europeans, as well as Brazilian singers, who have chosen to make the lovely seaside village their home.

Caraíva

Time really has stood still in this tranquil village without electricity or

WHALE WATCHING

Magnificent female humpback whales and their newborn calves can be seen between August and October off the coast of Bahia, particularly around the archipelago of Abrolhos, which is now a national marine park. Brazil only ended all whaling operations in 1985, and humpback whales are now an endangered species. The Instituto Baleia Jubarte (Humpback Whale Institute, *www.baleiajubarte.com.br*) educates boat owners and crew around Abrolhos to protect the magnificent creatures, which are vulnerable to human and boat interference. Boats leave from the small town of Carvelas to the Parque Nacional Marinho de Abrolhos for day trips, as well as longer diving and fishing trips.

paved roads. Accessible only by boat along the coast, or by canoe along the Caraíva river, life is lived at a slow pace, with locals fishing and making handicrafts from wood and coconut. Walk along the wild beach or take a fishing boat to visit the Indian Reserve of Barra Velha.

SALVADOR (*CIDADE ALTA*)

Like Rio de Janeiro, Salvador was once the capital of Brazil; it is also set on a beautiful bay and is one of the world's most enchanting cities. Salvador is African to the core and its slave traditions are kept alive by the essentially Afro-Brazilian population here. The city's exquisite baroque churches, exotic rituals and heart-pounding rhythms combine to form a rich experience that is nothing short of intoxicating.

Pelourinho

The gold-filled churches and pastel-coloured mansions of the rich sugar barons were built up high to protect them from Indian attack. Pelourinho is the historical heart of the *cidade alta* (upper city) and a UNESCO World Heritage Site. Although a lot of money has been spent successfully renovating the area, the same investment has not been bestowed on the residents, and many are poor, hungry and sick. Begging in the street and pick-pocketing is still something to watch out for.

A Taste of Carnaval

There is a little bit of Carnaval almost every night of the week in Pelourinho, with dancing, drumming and live music in the streets and squares. Tuesday night is the big event, called *benção* (blessing) after the weekly

Good luck ribbons are a popular souvenir in Bahia

Pelourinho's colourful streets

church custom of giving bread to the hungry. On Sunday, **Olodum** – a big name from Carnaval – play their infectious African beats, and the all-girl drumming group **Didá** (*www.dida-salvador.com*) is not to be missed on Fridays.

Largo do Pelourinho

From the Terreiro de Jesus (*see below*), steeply sloping streets lead down to the Largo do Pelourinho, a small, triangular plaza named after the pillory where slaves were tied, humiliated and tortured until their blood ran onto the cobbles. The post was moved from the Terreiro de Jesus when the slaves' screams disrupted the lessons in the Jesuits' church and school.

The powder-blue **Casa de Jorge Amado** (*www.fundacaojorgeamado.com.br*) is the old house of Jorge Amado, who was perhaps Brazil's favourite author. Amado only died in 2001 and his old house, which he asked not to be made into a museum, is now a café and cultural centre.

The **Igreja Nosso Senhor do Rosário dos Pretos** was the only church where slaves were allowed to worship. There is a shrine to Anastácia Escrava, an Angolan slave princess who was muzzled as a torture that ended in death. On Tuesdays at 6pm there is a spirited service with drumming, singing and dancing.

Terreiro de Jesus

The two main squares of Praça da Sé and Terreiro de Jesus lie either side of the Catedral Basílica. Next door to the cathedral, the **Museu Afro-Brasileiro**

The mesmerising Igreja de São Francisco

CAPOEIRA

The hypnotic twang of the *berimbau* (a single-stringed bow) accompanies the acrobatic and balletic moves of two performers in a *roda* (circle). Slaves developed the ritualised, rhythmic movements as a way of disguising their martial art, whose name may have come from the word for castrated rooster. It was banned in Brazil until Mestre Bimba founded the first school of Capoeira and performed in front of Getúlio Vargas in 1937, who recognised it as a national sport and understood its educational and cultural role. Fundação Mestre Bimba (*Rua das Laranjeiras 1. Tel: (71) 3322 0639*) is the best place to take lessons and watch performances, usually daily at 6pm.

(*Tel: (71) 3321 2013. www.ceao.ufba.br/mafro. Open: Mon–Fri 9am–6pm, Sat & Sun 10am–5pm. Admission charge*) has an interesting collection of Orixás and other items relating to candomblé as well as African art in various media.

The **Convento e Igreja de São Francisco** (*Tel: (71) 3322 6430. Open: Mon–Sat 8am–noon & 2–6pm, Sun 7am–noon*) is one of the most extravagantly baroque churches in the Americas. Gold literally covers the interior, which is also decorated with *azulejos* (traditional Portuguese tiles) and rosewood carvings, all the work of slave labour.

SALVADOR (*CIDADE BAIXA*)

The 'lower city' is largely the commercial district. Beyond are Barra and its urban beach which was, until Pelourinho was revitalised, the place to stay. Although a little down at heel, it is still worth a visit for its lighthouse and fort. From Barra, Avenida Oceánica

Capoeira disguised early beliefs (*see p88*)

links a series of beaches, many of which are polluted but have lively *barracas* (beach bars).

Feira de São Joaquim

On the waterfront by the ferry terminal of the same name is this open-air market which gives a real insight into local life. All kinds of fresh produce, from bleating goats to sausage-sized rolls of tobacco and slabs of just-hooked fish, are sold at the thousands of stalls set up every day except Sunday.

Igreja de Nosso Senhor do Bonfim

The Igreja do Bonfim, as everybody calls this church, was built in 1745 on the square of the same name and is an important centre for Candomblé (*see pp88–9*). Ribbons, known as *fitas*, are sold outside, supposedly granting a wish each of the three times it is tied to its owner's wrist. The ribbon should be allowed to fall off naturally – a process that can take months; cutting the ribbon is said to bring bad luck.

Inside, the Sala dos Milagres (Room of Miracles) is filled with touching visual requests – such as a photograph of an injured body, or a replica of a hurt limb – for anything from a football team win to the recovery of a dying child. There are also thanks for wishes granted, in the form of hand-written

The Elevador Lacerda provides sweeping views of the bay

notes, as well as watches, and keys to cars and houses.
Praça Senhor do Bonfim, Bonfim. Tel: (71) 3316 2196. Open: Tue–Sun 6.30–11.30am & 1.30–6pm. Free admission.

Mercado Modelo

The upper and lower city are linked by the **Elevador Lacerda** (known as the 'priests' hoist' after the Jesuits who once used it to transport building materials), which offers wonderful views of the bay. At the bottom, the handicrafts market of Mercado Modelo in the former customs house is touristy, but is a fun place to shop and people-watch.
Praça Vicsconde de Cairu 250. Open: Mon–Sat 9am–7pm, Sun 9am–2pm.

Street sellers

Throughout the city, and indeed the state, you can't miss the smiling faces of the women in huge white dresses, known as *Baianas de acarajé* (Bahian *acarajé* women) after the distinctive, traditional food they sell on the street. *Acarajé* is a fried bean dumpling served with *camarão* (tiny sun-dried shrimp) and *vatapá* (a shrimp, nut and coconut paste).

A *Baiana de acarajé* with her colourful creations

Candomblé

Sculpture of Oxóssi, an *orixá*, at the Catacumba Park in Rio de Janeiro

Although the African religious practice of Candomblé is dismissed by some as a cult, intellectuals, including Brazil's most famous author Jorge Amado and presidents such as Lula, recognise its social importance. Today, the African Candomblé is flourishing across Brazil, and even appearing in middle-class enclaves around the world.

Playing in the dark

Like the fighting/dancing art form Capoeira, Candomblé was born out of severe restrictions placed on the slave communities. Unable to freely practise their religion, they resorted to 'playing in the dark' as Capoeira is often described, worshipping after nightfall and diluting any African elements. Practitioners cleverly adopted Catholic forms of worship, making offerings at a *peji*, or altar, using bread as in communion and disguising their gods as Catholic saints. In this way, Olorum became the God figure, Oxala the representation of Jesus, and the Virgin Mary a disguise for Imenjá, the sea goddess honoured throughout the country on New Year's eve by Brazilians of all beliefs.

The devil's work?

Two million Brazilians declare Candomblé as their faith, but as many as 20 million people may practise it alongside Catholicism, the official religion. Although its traditional stronghold is Bahia, Candomblé ceremonies are also held all around the cities of Rio de Janeiro and São Paulo. Candomblé was banned in some parts of Brazil until as recently as the 1970s and is still regarded as backward, if not blasphemous, by certain less liberal sections of society. The strongest opposition comes from the fast-growing Pentecostal Church, although Candomblé followers have successfully sued against accusations of devil worship.

A dance to the gods

A Candomblé ceremony begins with an animal sacrifice in the morning, carried out by the high priest and priestess and unseen by the general congregation. The word literally means 'a dance in honour of the gods', and music – particularly drumming – and colourful costumes are integral elements. As a call to the spirits, practitioners, who are always women, fall into a state of frenetic trance. After the ceremony, food is handed out and dancing usually continues until late into the night.

Thank your lucky stars

In Candomblé, everyone has one or two *orixás* (elemental spirits reflecting an aspect of god) that determine their personality from birth, rather like the star signs of the zodiac. They are determined by Jogo de Buzios, a shell 'game' performed by a priest. Each of the *orixás* has its own personality and favourite offerings, which are given to say 'thank you' or to make a request.

Open to visitors

Ceremonies last around three hours, and are usually held at *terreiros* (temple compounds or houses), of which there are around 2,000 in Salvador. Visitors are normally permitted to attend, but dress respectfully and wear white or light colours to avoid offending any of the *orixás*. These are religious ceremonies, so don't take photographs or expect one highlight after the other. Agencies in Pelhourinho have been known to sell tickets for staged experiences; ask instead at the tourist office for contact details of local *terreiros*, most of which are out in the suburbs. Or, better still, go to Cachoeira for the most authentic experience of all.

Excursion: Baía de Todos Santos (Bay of All Saints)

*Salvador sits on the 60 km (37-mile) wide Baía de Todos Santos, the largest bay in Brazil. What looks like the mainland on the other side of the calm water is in fact the long island of Itaparica, just 14km ($8^2/_3$ miles) away and an easy boat trip. Travel across the bay by boat, or take a trip around it overland, visiting the two lovely, relaxed historic towns of São Félix and Cachoeira, by taxi, bus or with one of the fascinating trips offered by Terra Brazil (*www.terra-brazil.com*).*

Itaparica

This island is very popular with Brazilians who flock to the beaches here. There are lots of holiday homes and the accommodation tends to be expensive so it is best avoided at weekends. In the main town of Itaparica bikes can be hired for rides through the peaceful streets or to other parts of the island. Combi vans link all the main beaches, picking up and dropping off passengers anywhere along their route.

Boat trips

Pequena lanchas (small passenger boats) leave Salvador from near the Mercado Modelo throughout the day and land at Itaparica's Mar Grande (Big Sea), a relaxed town with a nice beach and some great *barracas* selling freshly caught crab and fish. Larger boats and catamarans leave from Terminal São Joaquim for Bom Despacho on Itaparica. Cruises sold in advance normally include hotel pick-up, with cocktails and entertainment on board a schooner. These organised trips usually stop at smaller islands on the way for snacks and souvenir shopping, before returning to Salvador for sunset and wonderful views of the city.

Recôncavo

The fertile land that follows the curve of Baía de Todos Santos takes its name from its concave shape. Here were once Brazil's most successful sugar and tobacco plantations, which created the wealth on which Salvador was built. The towns of the Recôncavo are sleepy spots, best explored by wandering their pretty, narrow streets. Santo Amaro, 60km (37 miles) from Salvador (along the BR-324 and BA-026), has some faded old mansions and churches, as well as a Saturday market.

Cachoeira

Forty kilometres (25 miles) west of Santo Amaro on the banks of the Paraguaçu river, this little city is one of the prettiest in Bahia and was its capital twice. Its lovely colonial centre includes several historic museums and churches as well as artisans' studios. The **Casa da Câmara e Cadeia** (1698) is the old prison that also once served as the seat of the Bahian government. **Pousada do Convento** (*Tel: (75) 3425 1716*), a former convent and the best place to stay, is next door to the **Convento e Igreja Nossa Senhora do Carmo** (1715) on Praça da Aclamação. Don't miss Candomblé here on Friday or Saturday night.

São Félix

Cachoeira is linked to its twin town on the opposite bank of the river, São Félix, by the fragile-looking steel **Dom Pedro II bridge** (1885). The **Centro Cultural Dannemann** on the riverfront (*Avenida Salvador Pinto 29. Tel: (75) 3425 2208. Closed: Mon. Free admission*) has exhibits relating to the production of local cigars – thought to be the finest in the world in the 18th century. From São Félix it is possible to continue around the western side of the bay, crossing the Ponte do Funil to Itaparcia and returning to Salvador by car ferry.

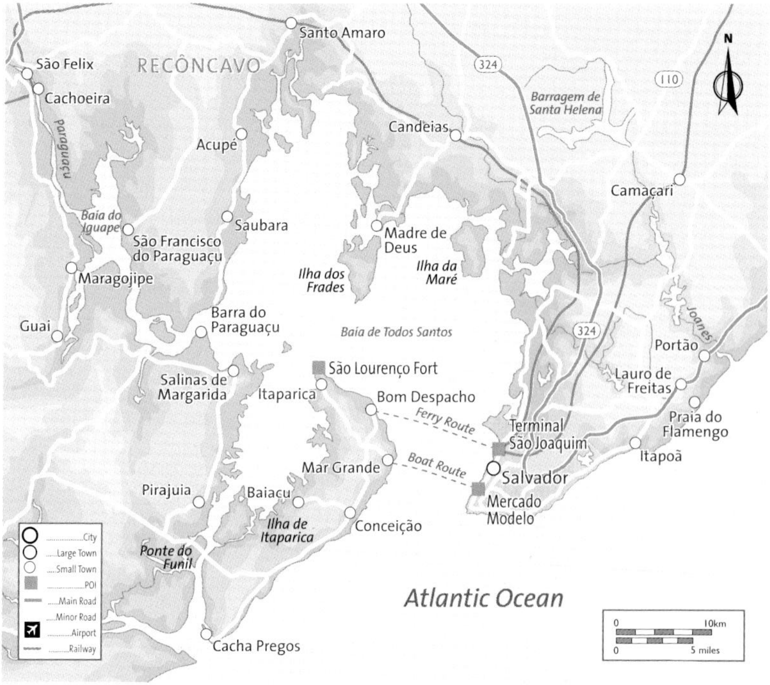

PRAIA DO FORTE

This fishing village, with a 12-km ($7^1/_2$-mile) long beach backed with coconut trees, is a peaceful, upmarket resort. Most of the land is owned by a forward-thinking businessman who created an eco-resort where cars and development are restricted. It is possible to visit Praia do Forte on a day trip from Salvador, but many visitors, particularly families, stay here as part of a package.

THE STRUGGLE OF A TURTLE

Incredibly, female turtles manage to find their way back across oceans to the beach where they were born. Between September and March under the protection of nightfall they scrape a hole in the sand with their front flippers and lay 100 or so ping-pong-ball-sized eggs. Eight weeks later, the baby turtles struggle to break through their shells and the sand and make their way to the sea. 35 years after that, the lucky ones will return to the same beach as adults – only one in a hundred make it – to repeat the cycle. Turtles are still killed for their meat and eggs in some parts of Brazil, but the fishermen in Praia do Forte have put an end to this practice.

Beach and nature

Although the waters can be rough enough for surfers, at low tide natural pools are carved by coral reefs that fill with tropical fish. Fishing, snorkelling and diving trips are all possible. The **Sapiranga Ecological Reserve** a little inland protects one of Brazil's last remnants of primary Atlantic rainforest where trails can be followed to spot monkeys and get to waterfalls. Near the Praia do Forte Resort Hotel, the **Timeantuba Bird Reserve** is best explored by canoe to see alligators and nearly 200 bird species. An enjoyable 3-km ($1^1/_2$-mile) walk out of town leads through forest reserve to the hilltop castle of **Castelo do Garcia d'Avila** (1552).

A baby turtle is given a helping hand

Projeto TAMAR turtle sanctuary

Five of the seven species of sea turtle in the world are found in Brazil. Pollution, industrial fishing and even the love of turtle soup have threatened them to the point of extinction. Next to the lighthouse on the beach, Projeto TAMAR has observation tanks and a small museum. It is a great success story, the flagship of a network of coastal projects that have released more

than three million turtle hatchlings to date.
Tel: (71) 676 1045.
www.projetotamar.org.br.
Open: 9am–5.50pm.
Admission charge, children under five free.

Costa do Sauípe

This man-made resort (*www.costadosauipe.com.br*) is, no matter what you make of it, an extraordinary achievement. Out of an empty stretch of 'Coconut Coast', five international luxury hotels, six themed *pousadas* and an artificial colonial village, complete with street food sellers, have been constructed.

Most of Costa's visitors never leave; all drinks, food and entertainment are included in the gated complex, although some visitors may venture out on a day or night trip to Salvador. Sports facilities are impressive; there is an 18-hole golf course, a windsurfing lake, nautical sports centre and professional-standard tennis courts. The resort is not without its critics, but it does contribute to local environmental and social programmes.

Fishing boats at rest in Praia do Forte

Carnaval

Most of us have seen the Brazilian Carnaval parades that are projected onto television screens around the world, but nothing can prepare a Carnaval virgin for the raw emotion, the sweat, smiles and tears of the real thing, when your hair seems to stand on end and you do believe Carnaval really is the greatest show on earth.

Sambadrome and the streets

Rio's festivities were taken off the streets and put into the Sambódromo (Sambadrome) in 1984. This is a move that cities such as São Paulo have mimicked, but elsewhere Carnaval is still very much a street festival, with even more intimate festivals taking place in outlying villages (*see 'Festivals and events', pp20–21*).

A practical approach

Accommodation prices quadruple and rooms are only sold as five- or even seven-day packages; almost everywhere gets fully booked, so reserve ahead as far as possible. Rip-offs abound, the best restaurants fill up and many tourist attractions close. Consider travelling the week before Carnaval for a much more relaxed and inexpensive experience; you can still see the rehearsals and soak up much of the atmosphere. The committed who are prepared to travel

Astride a giant horse in Rio's Sambódromo

Carnival dancers in Bahian costume

and have the stamina can take in all three of the main Carnaval celebrations in one week.

A glitzy affair: Rio

At the heart of Carnaval are the Escolas de Samba (Samba Schools) that parade in the Sambódromo in Rio. For an unforgettable experience, visitors can buy a costume (well in advance) and take part in the extravaganza. The alternative is to buy a spectator's ticket, the most expensive of which are US$1,000 for a space (not a seat), with the white élite in a *camarote* (box) served by waiters in black tie. *Blocos* (blocks) are groups dressed to a theme that perform in different neighbourhoods to all; Ipanema with its drag queens is a popular spot.

In the weeks running up to Carnaval, it is possible to watch schools rehearsing throughout the city. In addition, the Cidade do Samba (City of Samba), billed as 'Carnaval all year long' (*Avenida Rodrigues Alves. Tel: (21) 2213 2503. www.cidadedosambarj.com.br*), has behind-the-scenes workshops where costumes and floats are made, as well as nightly shows.

Back to basics: Salvador

Many Brazilians dismiss Rio's Carnaval as *fantasia* (fantasy), and will advise you to go to Salvador for Carnaval, where it is still relatively non-commercial. There are no semi-naked women in feathered, sequinned costumes. In fact, there are few costumes; many local people do not even have shoes, but everyone seems to fall into the frenzy of African drums that is a real celebration of black heritage. The parade of *trio elétricos* (trucks with enormous speakers) is made up of three different circuits. Either buy an *abadá* (outfit allowing you to join a Carnaval group) in advance, or just enjoy being *pipoca* (popcorn) – an onlooker.

Local rhythms: Pernambuco

Carnaval in the far northeast is altogether more folkloric than those further south, with *frevo*, a local rhythm, featuring prominently. In the city of Recife, celebrations are big and brash. African-influenced *troças* and *maracatus* are the main event, while in Olinda celebrations are overshadowed by enormous, papier-mâché puppets.

The northeast

In this book the 'northeast' refers to the bulge on Brazil's easternmost tip – from Recife around the country's nose to the 'brow' of Fortaleza. The entire coast is fringed with beach upon beach under enormous blue skies. It was the first part of the country to be colonised by Portugal on any scale and it is also the closest to Europe. With much shorter flying times than the south of Brazil, cheap package deals to here, particularly from the UK, have really taken off.

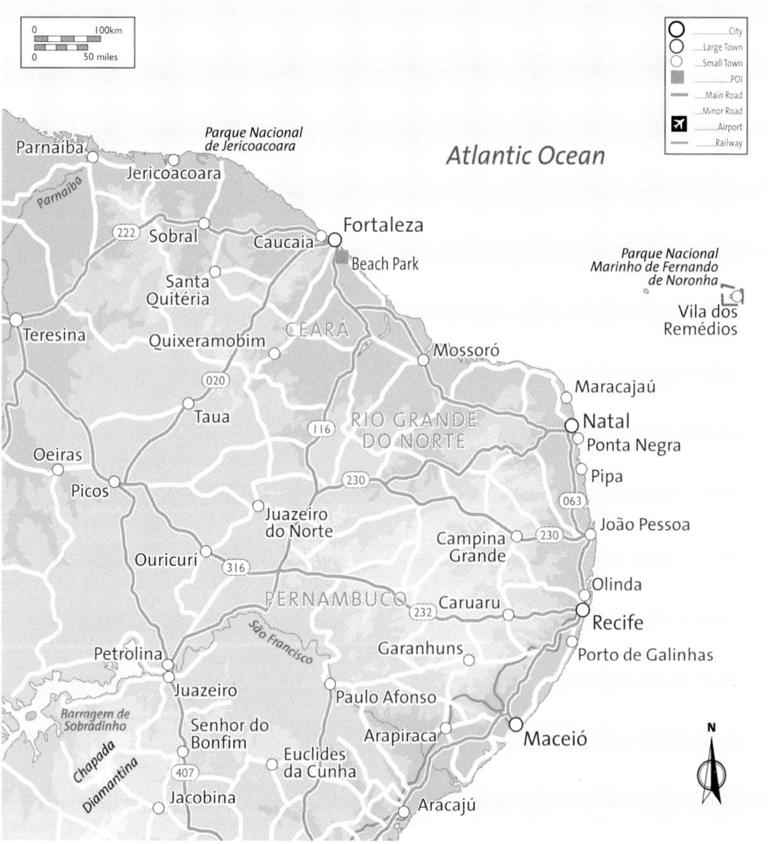

Calm pools and deep reefs are a feature of the northeast

Inland are some of Brazil's poorest communities where, for example, infant mortality rates are comparable to Africa and India. The Portuguese imported large numbers of slaves to work the sugar plantations. Subsequently, poverty, drought and poor soil drove inhabitants of the northeast to travel throughout Brazil in search of work, and their influence is felt all over the country, although the African heritage in this area remains particularly strong.

Visitors should try to get into the interior (*see 'Getting away from it all', p124*), where the semi-arid *sertão* (backlands) is covered with *caatingas* (scrubland), gouged with canyons and dotted with cacti. The rewards are spirited, kindly locals and a distinct, rich culture. Here, *vaqueiros* (cattlemen) roam the land, and local festivals are celebrated with a fervour not found elsewhere. This part of Brazil is a centre for arts and crafts and also the focus for the foot-tapping rhythm of *forró*.

Despite its distance from the powerhouses of Rio and São Paulo in the south, the northeast is in many ways the heart of Brazil. This region is the birthplace of the country's industry and cornerstone to its crafts. Come Carnaval, giant puppets stalk the streets and crisscrossing parades throw up live sound clashes, as euphoric residents lend their unique flair to this fabulous festival.

PERNAMBUCO

Recife, the industrial capital of Pernambuco state, is overwhelmingly modern, with a compact historical centre and a brash, snaking, urban beach. Once a Dutch port, Recife was named after its long reefs, while its canals have led it rather hopefully to be called the 'Venice of Brazil'. Olinda (meaning 'how beautiful') is the original state capital, a delightful little colonial town whose charming *pousadas* make it a much more desirable base than Recife. For beaches, head to Porto de Galinhas. The 'Port of Chickens' was so-called because, after the prohibition of slavery, the phrase 'there are new chickens in the port' was passed around as code to announce the arrival of human contraband.

Olinda

The cobbled streets of Olinda's historic centre, a UNESCO site 7km (4$^1/_3$ miles) north of Recife, were made for walking. Climb up to **Alta da Sé** for an impromptu crafts and food market and great views of the pretty rooftops. Rua do Amparo is one of the prettiest streets, lined with shops and restaurants. **Casa dos Bonecos Gigantes** (*No 45. Tel: (81) 3439 2443. Open: Mon–Fri 8am–noon*) is the 'House of the Giant Puppets', created

Some of Olinda's pretty houses date back to the 16th century

by Botelho, the 'father' of the 4-m (13 ft) high figures which form such a big part of Olinda's Carnaval. The **Museu de Arte Contemporânea (MAC)** may be of little interest now, but historically was once a prison for those who 'conspired' against the Catholic church; the first floor was reserved for 'blacks, creoles and witches'. The nearby **Mercado da Ribeira** was where slaves were traded and is now a market for handicrafts bought and sold. Lovers of all things ecclesiastical will delight in Olinda's numerous churches, particularly the elaborate woodcarving in **Mosterio de São Bento** on the street of the same name.

Porto de Galinhas

The main attraction of this area 60km (37 miles) south of Recife is the beautiful stretch of beach with clear, fish-filled tidal pools created by a long rib of coastal reef. Traditional fishing boats known as *jangadas* take visitors out to them in an almost idyllic scene. Although its tiny centre, consisting of a few streets around the main square, remains relatively untouched, the one-time fishing village is being increasingly developed.

Recife

The colourful colonial houses of Rua da Bom Jesus in Recife Antigo (Old Recife) have been restored to become one of the city's highlights. Tables spill out onto the pavements from the bars and restaurants, live music fills the air at weekends and there is a Sunday market of local handicrafts. Three bridges connect Old Recife to the commercial, yet still historic, district of Santo Antônio. Head to the cobbled plaza of Pátio de São Pedro with its glorious cathedral of the same name, where there is often live music in the evening. The 7-km ($4^1/_3$-mile) beach of Boa Viagem is shadowed by skyscrapers, as well as sharks; since 1992 there have been more than 50 attacks, some say caused by environmental degradation when a new port closed off two freshwater estuaries.

Jagandas transport both fish and tourists in Porto de Galinhas

PARQUE NACIONAL MARINHO DE FERNANDO DE NORONHA

This tiny archipelago, 545km (339 miles) from Recife in the middle of the Atlantic Ocean, is the visible part of a sub-sea volcanic mountain range. Most of it is protected as a marine national park, home to schools of dolphins, rays, tropical fish, sharks and barracudas and offering some of the best diving in the world.

History

The Dutch, French and Portuguese fought over this New-World staging post, but it was subsequently forgotten until it became a telegraph relay station. Fernando de Noronha was also once a penal colony, and, during World War II, a US naval base.

Practicalities

Tourism here is strictly managed by IBAMA, the environmental protection arm of the Brazilian government. Upon arrival, all visitors must pay TPA (Environmental Preservation Tax) which is around R$200 for a seven-day visit. Flights from Recife take around 90 minutes (*see 'Getting around', pp133–4*). Tourism being the only real industry on the island, there are plenty of *pousadas*, and many locals rent out rooms, but finding a bed can be difficult in the peak months of January and February. Bring everything you will need (cash, medicines, sunblock, etc.) as facilities are few and prices here reflect the cost of air freight from the mainland.

A deserted beach in the national park

The 'two brothers' stand guard

Diving

One of the biggest attractions here is the clear water teeming with coral sea life. Visibility is sometimes as much as 50m (164ft) and the average temperature is 26°C (79°F). Around the island there are 19 dive sites, 12 on the sheltered Mar de Dentro.

The island

In a country blessed with beautiful islands, Fernando de Noronha is outstanding. The lush inland vegetation gives way to 16 beaches, guarded by towering rocky outcrops where forts were built in days gone by. In the northeast of the island is the main settlement of Vila dos Remédios where dune buggies can be hired to get around. The beaches on Mar de Dentro (the side facing the mainland) are relatively calm, with those on Mar de Fora that face the Atlantic more windswept.

Praia Cacimba do Padre is one of the island's most stunning beaches, with 0.9km (1/2 mile) of golden sands over 150m (500ft) wide in places. To the south is **Baía dos Porcos** (Bay of Pigs), guarded by the twin outcrops of Dos Irmãos (Two Brothers) and the ruins of an 18th-century fort. Pools of green, sparkling water are backed by steep cliffs alive with tropical plants. Access is by boat or across the rocks from **Praia Cacimba**. South of here is **Praia Sancho**, a sheltered and secret little sandy cove with access down a staircase built into a crevice.

Swimming in the next bay south is prohibited as **Baía dos Golfinhos** is reserved for dolphins; hundreds of them gather early each morning to play

Parque das Dunas nature reserve

before heading out to sea to find food. Close to Vila dos Remédios, **Praia da Conceição** is the place to watch the sun set, framed by the monolithic Morro do Pico rising from the forest.

On the Atlantic side, **Praia do Leão** is a wild, deserted stretch of sand where sea turtles come ashore to lay eggs between January and June.

NATAL AND RIO GRANDE DO NORTE

The 400-km (249-mile) coastline of the small state of Rio Grande do Norte is effectively one long beach of blinding white sand interrupted by the occasional fishing village. Clear lagoons, dense forest and towering dunes back the mostly peaceful beaches where dolphins and sea turtles can be spotted in the water. This state is much drier than those further south and it enjoys almost year-round sunshine.

Beaches

Day trips to the fishing village of Maracajaú, 60km (37 miles) north of Natal, are offered in the city. The many *parrachos* (reefs) make it a wonderful spot for diving, and there is also sand-dune riding. North of here are beautiful, largely deserted beaches waiting to be discovered.

Natal: Cidade do Sol (City of Sun)

Natal is a clean, modern city and the state capital. The star-shaped **Forte dos Reis Magos** (Fort of the Wise Kings, 1598) stands on the original site of the city, on the sands of Praia Forte next to the Potengi river. In the **Centro do Turismo** (*Rua Aderbal de Figueiredo 980. Open: 8am–7pm*) the old prison cells have been converted into stalls selling handicrafts as well as the tourist office.

Natal's beaches are decidedly urban,

Inside the courtyard of the Forte dos Reis Magos

Heading to Pipa in a dune buggy

but the lovely beach of Ponta Negra (*see below*) is easily accessed via the **Via Costeira**, a 10-km/6¼-mile road with cycle path, sandwiched by large luxury hotels and the nature reserve of **Parque das Dunas** (*Tel: (84) 201 3985. Open: Tue–Sun 8am–6pm. Guided trails: call ahead for booking. Admission charge*).

Pipa

Pipa is a popular but relaxed resort, which can be reached on a day trip from Natal. There are plenty of *pousadas* and restaurants here – many of them foreign owned – and some of the best nightlife on the whole coast (*www.pipa.com.br* has more information). There is good surf off the lovely, if sometimes crowded, beach, as well as boat and canoe rides. Buggies and horses can be ridden along the sand, and dune trails lead through an ecological sanctuary with Atlantic forest.

Ponta Negra

In the crook at the southern end of the Via Costeria is the sheltered beach of this one-time fishing village. Today Ponta Negra is a lively spot full of *pousadas*, restaurants and bars and is particularly busy at weekends. The 120-m (394-ft) high dune of Morro de Careca (Bald Man's Hill) at the southern end is closed to visitors to protect it from sliding into the sea.

Rota do Sol

The 'Sun Route' leads south from Natal along the RN-063 to Pipa, 85km (53 miles) away. On the beach at **Pirangi**, 14km ($8^2/_3$ miles) down the coast, is the biggest cashew tree in the world; its lazy, sprawling crown, more than $^1/_2$km ($^1/_3$ mile) in circumference, looks more like a forest than a single tree.

At **Barra de Tabatinga**, 26km (16 miles) further on, is a long stretch of sand where a reef breaks the water to form shallow rock pools; on top of the cliff is a lookout from where you may be lucky enough to see dolphins.

Tibaú do Sol, just 5km (3miles) north of the beach at Pipa between the calm waters of Guaraíras Lagoon and the Atlantic Ocean, is an Indian name meaning 'between two waters' and is a beautiful spot where the sand is sheltered by the high cliffs.

Bald Man's Hill in Ponta Negra

Lula and the landless

From its beginnings as a Portuguese colony, Brazil has been fixed on the idea that the vast wealth of the land exists for the benefit of the few. This notion went unchallenged for centuries, despite independence, and throughout the 20th century, regardless of which army general or civilian politician was in charge. So it was with downright horror (and despite their best efforts and countless millions spent) that Brazil's ruling class watched the Workers Party win the 2002 general election.

A fly in the ointment

Here was a party dedicated to changing the status quo, and, worse still, at their head was a former shoeshine boy from an illiterate 'peasant' family in the poor northeastern state of Pernambuco. When he was a boy, Lula's mother took the family south to São Paulo. As a teenager working in a car factory, he lost his finger when an exhausted co-worker fell asleep at the machine they were operating. He became a union leader, but disliked politics, and it was only endless injustice that drove him, at the age of 35, to join the foundation of the Workers Party.

Everything and nothing

Before Lula came Cardoso, and before him the smooth-talking Fernando Collor, elected in 1989 in the country's first truly free and universal elections. When Lula took over, little had improved. Five million rural families had no land whatsoever, no jobs and no food. At the same time, the wealthy élite owned three quarters of Brazil's arable land – an area the size of India – with over one third of it underused and untended.

The Landless Workers Movement, known as the MST from its Portuguese initials, has sought to change this on the basis that the Brazilian constitution allows for unproductive land to be expropriated for social use. By setting up roadside camps on the edge of the unused estates, they have drawn attention to their plight. At the same time, the MST (set up in 1984 as a cross between a community action group and rural trade union) is educating tens of thousands of children in its own schools, arming thousands of young people with labour skills, and feeding the poor in its community kitchens.

A demonstration by MST supporters

Progress

Lula is the MST's natural ally, and was elected on some bold promises, many of which have not been entirely fulfilled. He pledged ten million new jobs, but only four million have been created. Instead of 400,000 families settled on new land, the figure is only 235,000; and of the poorest 120 million people who were promised health care, just 70 per cent now have free hospitals, clinics and doctors. Compared to the track record of traditional politicians, these 'failures' rank as astonishing successes, all the more so because Lula has cannily worked to maintain foreign investment. In contrast, the firebrand tactics of Hugo Chavez in neighbouring Venezuela are threatening to undermine the revolution there.

Brazil's masses recognised Lula's shortcomings, but also the progress made in his first four years, when they narrowly re-elected him in 2006. The leadership of the MST has taken the same view, though in his second term Lula will be pressed to do even more to combat the crippling international debt and the multinationals that still control most of Brazil's land.

FORTALEZA

Named after the fort built by the Dutch in 1649, this city was eventually colonised by the Portuguese after fierce resistance from the Indians. Today it is a modern metropolis with a central grid system dotted with green squares, a bustling central market and hulking high-rises. But most people visit this state capital of Ceará for its many glorious beaches.

The city of 'the virgin with the honeyed lips'

José de Alencar wrote the classic romantic novel *Iracema* (1865) about the doomed love affair between an Indian girl and a Portuguese colonist. There are five long-legged, big-breasted statues of Iracema, who gives that beach its name, in the city. The 1908

Beach Park near Fortaleza – Brazil's biggest water park

DRAGONS OF THE SEA

The Centro Cultural Dragão do Mar (Dragon of the Sea Cultural Centre) honours the 19th-century activist Francisco José do Nascimento, who lost his job as Fortaleza's harbour pilot on joining the Black Abolitionist Movement. He motivated the local *jangadeiros* to refuse to carry slaves, and Ceará become Brazil's first state to free all slaves in 1884. Nascimento had sailed in his *jangada* to Rio to make his case, a treacherous 3,000-km (1,865-mile) journey. In 1941, four fishermen repeated the trip to demand equal workers' rights, inspiring Orson Welles to make a film. The voyage was re-enacted again in 1994 to protest about fishermen's rights and the environment. Today, the *jangadeiros* and their vessels continue as a symbol of the power, beauty and poverty of the northeast.

Teatro José de Alencar (*Tel: (85) 3101 2596. Open: Mon–Fri 9am–5pm*) on the square of the same name commemorates the author. The cast-iron structure was shipped over from Scotland and Burle Max designed the gardens of this magnificent classical concert venue.

Beaches

The unclean waters of Fortaleza's central beaches are not suitable for swimming. However, **Meireles**, where most of the upmarket hotels are located, is a pleasant spot with palm trees, beach huts and the long promenade Avenida Beira Mar. Join its early-evening strollers and roller skaters and take a look at its nightly handicrafts market. *Jangadeiros* (named after their rustic sailing rafts, *jangadas*, traditionally made of tree trunks) leave from Meireles to take tourists to nearby beaches.

A couple of kilometres or so east around the headland is the 4.8-km (3-mile) long **Praia do Futuro**, with cleaner, if rougher, water and 35-m (115-ft) sand dunes. *Barracas* (palm-roofed beach huts) dot the sands patrolled by enthusiastic hawkers, and there is sometimes live music in the evening.

About 6km (3¾ miles) further on is **Praia Porto das Dunas**, with surfing, water sports and **Beach Park**, an enormous water park (*Tel: (85) 4012 3000. www.beachpark.com.br. Open: 11am–5pm most days*).

West of Meireles, **Iracema's** 19th-century mansions and resident poets are rather aged now, but the city beach area still has a faintly bohemian air. Visit the **Ponte dos Ingleses** for sunset and then spend the evening at the bars and restaurants around the pier and **Centro Cultural Dragão do Mar** (*Avenida Dragão do Mar 81. Tel: (85) 3488 8600. www.dragaodomar.org.br*).

Cumbuco, 30km (18⅔ miles) north of Fortaleza, is a lovely beach surrounded by dunes and lagoons. Swing in a hammock under a palm tree, take a thrilling dune buggy ride to the clear waters of **Parnamirim** lagoon or visit the unspoilt sands of **Cauípe**, 8km (5 miles) away.

The Centro Cultural Dragão do Mar's planetarium lights up the night sky

Tour: Dune buggy adventure

The whole coast from Natal to Fortaleza is awash with spectacular sand dunes, though perhaps the most beautiful are at Genipabu, close to Natal. Hire a dune buggy for an exhilarating trip across this incongruous landscape where desert dromedaries relax on the beach silhouetted against the blue ocean. The route along the shoreline involves some tricky river-bed crossings, and it can sometimes pay to have an experienced driver if you are not confident.

Allow a full day for the trip.

Start at the Praia do Forte, the beach to the north of Natal, just 5km (3 miles) from the centre.

Praia do Forte

This is a pebble beach and the site of the well-preserved Forte dos Reis Magos (Fort of the Wise Kings). The fort was completed in 1598 on the twelfth day of Christmas, 6 January. Its position at the mouth of the Rio Potengi afforded a lookout for Dutch attacks from the sea and Indian attacks from the river.

Cross the Potengi river to reach the next beach, 20km ($12^1/_2$ miles) from the city.

Praia da Redinha

The Festa do Caju is celebrated here in early January and the Festa de Nossa Senhora dos Navegantes (procession of boats) on 20 January.

From this beach, it is another 5km (3 miles) to the most spectacular dunes of the trip.

Parque Ecológico Dunas de Genipabu

The park was set up to protect the shifting dunes here. Only drivers licensed by the tourist board are allowed onto these slopes due to the danger of sliding sands (to buggies and to the environment). The adventurous should ask for a ride *com emoção* (with emotion). The fixed dunes at Genipabu are open to all drivers, but as a consequence they can get busy, as does the beach itself.

Genipabu

This is a pleasant fishing village, where you will be guaranteed a decent fish lunch.

Drive just 8km (5 miles) north from here to Pitangui beach, which is usually much quieter than Praia Genipabu.

Pitangui

The beach is wide and long enough to get up to 60km/h (37mph), and this is a great location for speeding through the surf.

Continuing north along the shore for 6km (3¾ miles) brings you to Praia Jacumã.

Praia Jacumã

This is a fun beach surrounded by trees where you can stop off for a spot of *arobunda*. This involves climbing to the top of a dune where a cable has been suspended 200m (656ft) down to the surf line. Strap into the suspended seat and leap off the edge for a thrilling ride through the sky. A few *reais* should be more than enough to convince the locals to let you have a go.

To get to Muriú, you must cross the Ceará-Mirim river. For a small fee, locals blithely take cars and buggies across the water on their makeshift rafts, while tourists hold their breath.

Muriú

The seas here conceal shallow coral that is perfect for snorkelling, or if the winds are up, kite-surfing, a growing sport here.

For the return to Natal, it is possible to take the highway back from here.

Take an open-air trip through this dazzling landscape

The Amazon

For now at least, no river is larger, no forest so green and nowhere so plentiful. The Amazon has it all: giant snakes and spiders, thousand-year-old trees, fish of every shape and size, butterflies the size of bats and birds of any colour you can think of. The sights and sounds of the Amazon are unique, from the torrents of mixing waters where pink river dolphins gather to play, to the gangs of marauding monkeys that spring from branch to branch. To visit this wondrous collusion of intertwined ecosystems is a privilege.

From Belém on the Atlantic coast, the forest spreads south, north and far west, practically across the entire continent into Colombia and Peru. In the Andean foothills, near Lake Titicaca in the south of Peru, the river begins as a trickle, but is an unstoppable slow-moving behemoth when it reaches Belém many weeks later.

Belém is 2,500km (1,555 miles) from Rio, a six-hour flight, but this is just the start of an Amazonian odyssey. Several days upriver is Manaus, the old capital of the rubber boom, where stately

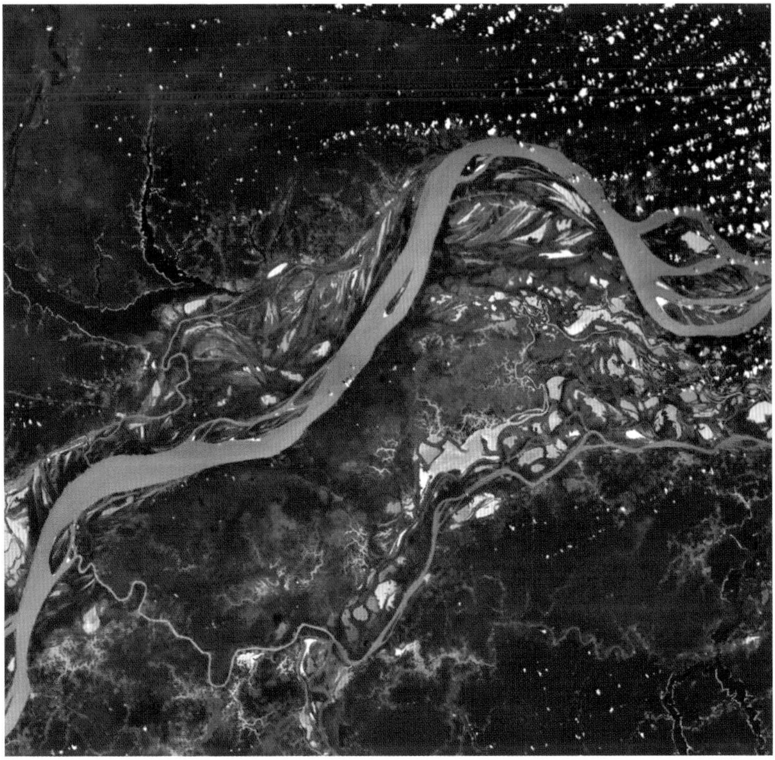

Amazon river flowing through the rainforest

mansions and an opera house worthy of Milan are testament to the decadent days when even horses drank vintage wines. Further upriver are idyllic eco-lodges, offering unforgettable jungle treks and midnight canoe trips.

History

The Amazon has given much. For thousands of years, it nourished all creatures great and small. It gave shelter to the scattered Stone-Age tribes who crossed the land bridge from North America. It gave up those tribes to disease and slavery when the Spanish and Portuguese arrived. In the Victorian age, it fed the industrial world's hunger for the new miracle material; vulcanised rubber. It furnished the world in tropical hardwood, its animals died in European zoos and its bowels gave up gold, oil, gas and minerals. Throughout it all, it has kept the planet breathing. The Amazon has much to offer, but we cannot afford to take more.

BELÉM

At the mouth of the Amazon river is Belém, the capital of the state of Pará. Around two million people live in this frontier city, which expanded during the 19th-century rubber boom. Before the rubber, exotic spices like vanilla and cinnamon and animal skins passed through the port, and merchants got rich in the process. A trip to the Amazon is a once-in-a-lifetime experience, so before heading into the jungle, take the opportunity to become acquainted with Belém's fascinating colonial history.

Belém's colonial past

Mercado Ver-o-Peso

The **Mercado Ver-o-Peso** (literally 'see-the-weight market') is over 100 years old. Its name derives from its former role as customs house, when merchandise was weighed by the authorities before being loaded onto boats. The market today is sprawling and colourful with over 2,000 stands selling traditional Indian cures for impotency, jealousy, arthritis, and anything else you can imagine. Amazonian delicacies and fragrant fruits such as *muruci* (a berry that makes great ice cream) and *taperebá* (java plum) are a treat for the senses.

Avenida Boulevard Castilhos França, Centro. Open: 8am–6pm.

Shopping Amazon-style

Museu Paraense Emílio Goeldi

One of the prime attractions in Belém affords a chance to learn about Amazon cultures and wildlife. The **Museu Paraense Emílio Goeldi** opened in 1866 and houses over 800 species of trees and 600 animals, many on the brink of extinction. There are also thousands of ceramic artefacts on show, some dating from the very beginnings of the human history in South America.

Avenida Magalhães Barata 376, São Brás. Tel: (91) 3219 3369. Open: 9am–5.30pm. Admission charge.

Theatro da Paz

Some sense of the huge wealth that flowed through this city can be gained by a visit to the **Theatro da Paz**. Inaugurated in 1878 and modelled after La Scala in Milan, this theatre and opera house reopened in 2002 after

A mix of grand buildings and shabby streets in Belém

substantial restoration. It hosts concerts, theatrical performances, art exhibitions and festivals. Visitors can also take guided tours by arrangement. *Rua da Paz, Centro. Tel: (91) 4009 8750. www.theatrodapaz.com.br. Open: Tue–Fri 9.30–11am, 12.30–2.30pm & 4–5pm, Sat 9am–7pm.*

Ilha de Marajó

From Belém, it is a three-hour boat trip across the Amazon estuary to the world's largest river island. The lowlands of Marajó, which is the size of Switzerland, become waterlogged from January to June, and are perfect grazing lands for huge herds of water buffalo. The wetlands are also home to sloths, monkeys and capybaras, plus piranha and arapaima (the world's biggest freshwater fish). For those in a rush, Marajó can also be reached by air taxi.

On Ilha de Marajó, buffaloes pull carts in a throwback to days gone by, and the mounted police ride these lumbering animals in place of horses. The buffalo exudes a hypnotic beauty and a rare sense of peace, and visitors should take the opportunity to get close, and even ride one, at the **Fazenda Bom Jesus** (*Tel: (91) 3741 1243*). This large ranch, run by a vet who loves the animals, is close to the village of Soure, 40km (25 miles) north of Salvaterra, the island's main settlement.

A buffalo takes to the water

MANAUS

Manaus, the capital of Amazonas state, is a colonial city with a dark history. It was built on the back of impoverished *serengueiros* (rubber tappers), serving a lifetime of debt-servitude. They were forced to buy supplies from the rubber barons who owned the forests, and to sell their harvest of latex at rock-bottom prices.

Mercado Municipal

The Mercado Municipal was built during the city's belle époque in the style of the famous 'Les Halles' market of Paris. Imported wrought ironwork covers three warehouses selling fruit, vegetables, jewellery and crafts. Nearby are the floating docks, built by a Scotsman in 1902. This marvel of Victorian engineering enabled ships to dock regardless of the seasonal variation in river depth. With no roads in or out of Manaus, the docks double as a bus station, and there is a constant bustle of people getting on and off crafts of varying degrees of seaworthiness.
Rua dos Barés 46. Open: daily 8am–6pm.

Museu de Ciências Naturais da Amazônia

Time permitting, make a trip to this natural history museum on the outskirts of the city. Specimens include 2.5-m ($8^1/_4$-ft) long fish like the piraíba (a type of catfish), and some frighteningly large insects. With descriptions of exhibits in English, this is a good place to become acquainted with the creatures you will see in the jungle.

Estrada do Japones, Colônia Cachoeira Grande, Alexico. Tel: (92) 3644 2799. Open: Mon–Sat 9am–5pm.

Teatro Amazonas: A night at the opera

During the rubber boom, there was little for white women to do beyond taking tea and reading French fashion magazines. The finest dresses were shipped over from Paris (and back again for cleaning), but such finery deserved to be shown off, and the barons built the monumental Teatro Amazonas as a testament to their wealth. Almost everything in this opulent theatre was imported from Europe, with the exception of the floor and armchairs made of native hardwoods, which were sent to Europe to be polished and carved. The streets outside the theatre were laid with rubber so that the noise of horse-drawn carriages would not interrupt the opera.

Despite being 1,500km (930 miles) from the coast and in the depths of the Amazon jungle, the opera house attracted world-class performers. Even after the boom, Rudolf Nureyev and Margot Fonteyn both danced here, and, following years of restoration, the theatre hosts regular worthwhile performances and a renowned opera festival.

Praça São Sebastião.
Tel: (92) 622 1880.
Open: 9am–4pm.

A NEW BOOM

Rubber made Manaus, but in 1873 the English smuggled seeds out of the Amazon and took them to Malaysia. The plants flourished in this new climate, and the English were able to produce rubber at a fraction of the cost of the rubber produced in the Amazon. Manaus fell into decline, with a brief respite in World War II when Japan took control of Malay. By the 1960s the population of Manaus had dropped to 200,000 but has since mushroomed to two million, thanks largely to Brazil's military dictatorship. It introduced a free trade zone which has seen the likes of Honda and Samsung relocate to the jungle outpost.

The British-built floating harbour at Manaus

INTO THE JUNGLE

Belém is the capital of Pará state whose forests have borne the brunt of 20th-century exploitation. There are few lodges worth visiting in the region, though it is a good starting point for a river trip up to Manaus, cheaper, if several days slower, than flying. Manaus is the state capital of Amazonas, which covers the western portion of the Brazilian Amazon where the rainforest is comparatively intact. Head here for an authentic Amazon experience.

Jungle bolt holes

After a couple of days in Manaus, most visitors are itching to head deep into the jungle. For those who can afford it, one of the most spectacular (and family-friendly) ways to experience the Amazon is on a river cruise, with the possibility of travelling upstream from Manaus all the way to Iquitos in Peru (*see 'River expedition', pp120–21*).

For those with less to spend, a number of companies offer jungle lodge packages, including transfers from Manaus and all meals, but not alcoholic drinks. Lodges are usually located along one of the many *igarapés* (small channels) that form the river system; canoe trips by day and night, as well as overland excursions into the forest, are all normally part of the package.

Ariaú Amazon Towers

This is a large, long-established lodge with accommodation linked by wooden and concrete bridges. Easily accessible from Manaus, this is supposed to be a

Exploring the riverbanks

superlative way to enjoy the Amazon, but with whirlpool baths, helicopter rides and capacity for more than 300 guests, this is neither an intimate nor eco-friendly Amazon experience.
www.ariauamazontowers.com

Nature Safaris

Nature Safaris is a firm with a good reputation. They operate two lodges a fair distance from Manaus, and a guesthouse in the city itself. Their Amazon eco-lodge is located five hours from Manaus in the firm's own private reserve, with sixteen rooms and shared bathrooms, spread out over six floating platforms, with rustic thatched roofs. Guests can take their own canoes for a paddle, or go fishing for piranha and peacock bass with guides.
www.naturesafaris.com.br

Pousada Uakarí

In stark contrast to Ariaú Amazon Towers, Pousada Uakarí is made up of five floating cabins 200km (124 miles) from Manaus, and is designed to minimise impact on surrounding

JUNGLE BUNGLES

If you haven't booked a lodge or tour in advance, don't negotiate with touts at the airport. Head to the city and quiz other travellers and the tourist office about the best trips. Always insist on English-speaking guides, and try to meet them beforehand and check out their green credentials. For example, any guide that picks up animals encountered on a trip does not show true regard for wildlife.

Lodges like Mamirauá are basic but close to nature

ecosystems. Visitors can take a twelve-hour boat from Manaus, or fly into Tefé and take a two-hour boat transfer. The lodge is in the middle of the Mamirauá reserve, a protected habitat for a host of rare creatures, including the white uakari monkey, endemic to the region. Visitors will meet qualified field researchers and can choose from forest treks and river expeditions with paddle canoes (rather than motorboats which disturb the animals). The best time to visit this flooded forest world is from April to July, when monkeys and sloths feast on the ripe fruit.
www.mamiraua.org.br

Tour: River expedition

The best jungle lodges are far from civilisation, but there is only so far one can travel in a river canoe. A cruise along the Amazon opens up a wealth of possibilities, the chance to experience the river at flood and ebb, and to see many more of the region's habitats, each with its own collection of birds, mammals, fish and reptiles.

A once-in-a-lifetime trip from Manaus upriver through the triple border with Colombia and Peru and on through the Peruvian Amazon to Iquitos is a 1,600-km (994-mile) journey and will take in the region of one to two weeks depending on the package.

1 Manaus

Half an hour from town, the ebony flow of the Rio Negro collides with the lighter streams of the Rio Solimões in the famous '**meeting of the waters**'. The result looks like a giant swirling chocolate mousse and sounds like a food mixer amplified 100 times. The black waters are coloured by decaying plantlife and mud from the northern Amazon, the brown and cream by the rocky sediments of the Andes in distant Peru.

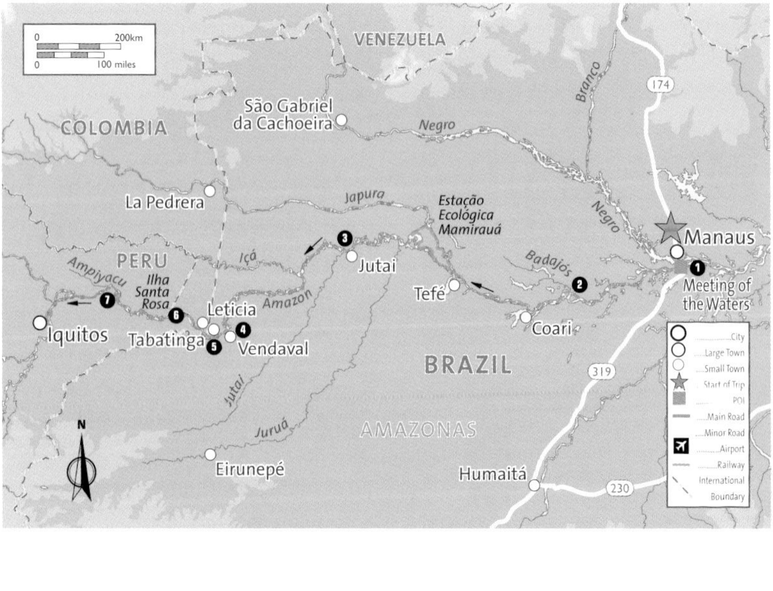

The 'meeting of the waters'

2 Rio Badajós

Where the tributary joins the Amazon, the waters make for fine fishing, and it is a wonderful spot for birdwatching too. Upriver is the small village of São Jão do Catua.

3 Rio Jutai

The black waters of the Rio Jutai, upriver from Lago Uara, are perfect for birdwatching, and swimming too. As night falls, take to a canoe to spot caimans lurking on the riverbank.

4 Vendaval

Go ashore at this village near Lago do São Paulo for a chance to sample life in a native Tikuna community, followed by a jungle hike.

5 Tabatinga

At the triple border, a visit to the town of Tabatinga on the Brazilian side and Leticia in Colombia is followed by a stop in the small Peruvian village of Santa Rosa. These different settlements offer an interesting picture of Amazonian life on the frontier of three different countries, all in one day.

6 Ilha Santa Rosa

Children have the chance to walk on water near here in a field of giant Amazonian water lilies, each the size of a coffee table.

7 Rio Ampiyacu

Go ashore here to bargain with the Boras and Huitos people for crafts. Native children will often approach the boat in canoes, or even swim out. Far from civilisation, they have practically nothing. If you can spare some clothes, toys or pens, wrap them up tight in a plastic bag and throw them over the side to be shared among the villagers.

The end of the line is the jungle town of Iquitos, as colourful in its own way as Manaus.

GETTING TO MANAUS

With few roads, the river is the local road system, and flights are costly, even for visitors. A cheaper option for those heading for Manaus is the ferry network from Belém via Santarém. In many ways, it is a better option than taking a large tourist boat up to Manaus; these are often characterless affairs, which navigate the central channels far from life on the riverbanks.

Amazon life

In 40 years' time, the Amazon will be dead, or alive. Such is the stark choice facing the world, although in reality there is no choice. The world needs the Amazon more than burger bars need beef, and certainly more than tycoons need tropical hardwood furniture. In the time it takes to say 'rainforest', another tree is felled. The challenge is to find some other source of income for the region's poor, and to rein in the loggers, ranchers, mining and mineral concerns that would rather put their profits first. Environmentally responsible tourism, with tangible benefits for local communities, is a start.

The wonders

The scale of the river, the fish, the forest and the forest dwellers is breathtaking. Elsewhere, the arapaima – a quarter of a tonne of scales and teeth – might attract attention, but skulking below the surface of the Amazon (which in places is as deep as a skyscraper), the world's biggest freshwater fish is commonplace. It needs more oxygen than it can get from the river alone, so must breathe air like a dolphin, especially when the river is at its lowest level. Then there is the world's largest rodent, the capybara, hunted by vultures when it wanders the riverbank, and by

Going ashore to meet and trade

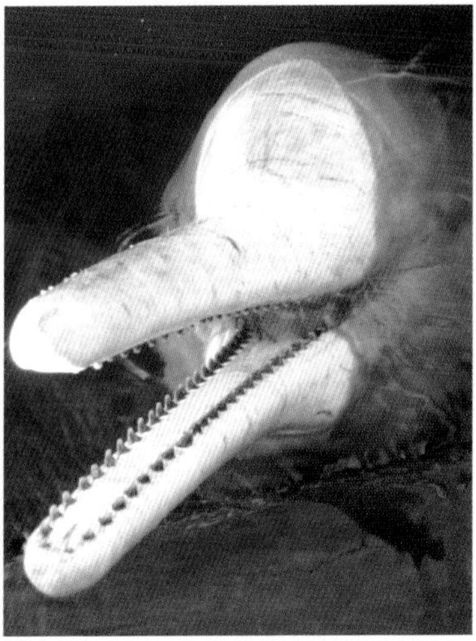

A river dolphin says hello

piranhas when it swims in the water. Reptiles such as river turtles and the caiman, a relative of the alligator, are best spotted at night, while gigantic anacondas that cling to branches above are best left alone.

Staying alive

The Nile may be the longest river, but the Amazon carries 40 times the volume – one fifth of the world's fresh water. This gigantic river system, and the forest around it, supports not only animal and plant life, but humans too. Despite incursions, there are still some tribes that have never had contact with Europeans, but these are few. As tribes retreated in the face of invasion, the conquerors pushed deeper into the jungle in search of new slaves. The modern result is *cabaclos*, of mixed Indian and Portuguese descent. They live in small settlements by the banks of the river, making a living from growing the manioc that is an important part of the Brazilian diet. Raised up on stilts, their homes become island villages when the rains come.

Rainy season

The rains are a time of plenty for all river creatures, and, since the piranha have smaller fish to fry, *cabaclo* children can safely swim in the river during rainy season. The forest is flooded to a depth of 10m (33ft) for 15km ($9^1/_3$ miles) either side of the main river channel. Fish find new hiding places, pursued by giant river otters, up to 2m ($6^1/_2$ft) in length, and pink Amazon river dolphins. Botos, as the dolphins are also known, are practically blind, but swimming in the muddy waters between the submerged tree trunks, sight is no advantage, and they use sonar to hunt. As the jungle floods, howler monkeys climb higher, but risk becoming lunch for the fearsome harpy eagle, its 15-cm (6-in) talons gleaming in the sun as it swoops down from the sky. It's a tough life, but the creatures of the Amazon are designed to cope with whatever their harsh environment throws at them. With us, it is a different matter.

Getting away from it all

Almost everyone in Brazil lives on the coast; venture even a little way inland and you are in another country. Here, in many respects, is the real Brazil, away from the pretty beaches and the tourist glitz. That said, there are secret beaches too; instead of heading for the most obvious stretch of sand, make the effort to travel a bit further, away from the tourist centres. Wherever possible, these have been highlighted in the 'Destination' guide, but coastal hideaways, by definition, change all the time, so always seek local advice.

Brazil is, of course, huge, so it is not always possible to 'get away from it all' quickly. Petrópolis and Chapada dos Guimarães are less than an hour from the nearest major city and easily visited in a day, but Chapada Diamantina, Jericoacoara and the *sertão* are all a good five hours away from significant civilisation and require several days to justify the journey. One of the main charms of all these destinations is the relaxed pace of life, so, wherever you choose to go, take things slowly to really enjoy them.

Escaping the crowds

Carriages line up outside the Museu Imperial in Petrópolis

Have the confidence to just stick a pin in a map and get to know 'ordinary' Brazil and some real people. In villages and towns where tourists of any nationality are rarely seen, you can get a real sense of Brazilian values. The hospitality, easy-going nature and sense of fun of the locals will resonate with you for a long time after you have returned home.

Petrópolis: Imperial mountain retreat

Petrópolis, in the cool hills north of Rio, was where the Portuguese royal family and its court went to escape the heat of the city. It is a lovely, relaxed spot, filled with history and surrounded by unspoilt nature. The journey through the Serra dos Órgãos ('Organ-pipe' Mountains, named after their distinctive shape) is one of the highlights. The road twists and turns through the dramatic scenery; sit on the left for the best view on the way up. When you get there, apart from the lovely town itself, you'll find that walking, horse-riding and climbing trips through lush vegetation dotted with waterfalls are all possible in the nearby Mata Atlântica.

Although the 'Imperial City' is only 70km ($43\frac{1}{2}$ miles) from Rio and easily manageable on a day trip by bus or organised tour, it is well worth hiring a car and spending the night in the lovely **Pousada da Alcobaça** (*www.pousadadaalcobaca.com.br*) on the edge of town. Petrópolis is a popular weekend getaway, so, if you can, visit during the week.

The compact historic centre cut through with pretty rivers and green squares is best explored on foot, or even

The wild canyons of Chapada Diamantina

horse and cart. Emperor Dom Pedro II founded Petrópolis in 1843; his summer palace is now the **Museu Imperial** (*Rua da Imperatriz 220. Tel: (24) 2237 8000. www.museuimperial.gov.br, Portuguese only. Open: Tue–Sun 11am–6pm. Admission charge*), perhaps Brazil's best museum and certainly its most visited. The crown jewels of Kings Pedro I and II are truly dazzling, and make sure to take a break at the Petit Palais, a French-style tearoom.

Stroll down Avenida Koeller to see the exteriors of the many fine old mansions and **Palácio Rio Negro** (*No 255*), the official summer residence of Brazil's presidents. Inventor and aviation pioneer Santos Dumont's house is now the delightful **Museu Casa de Santos Dumont** (*Rua do Encanto 22*), which he appropriately called 'the enchanted one'.

Parque Nacional da Chapada Diamantina: Brazil's 'Lost World'

The sleepy town of Lençóis, with its cobbled streets and pastel-coloured colonial buildings (six hours by road or a short flight inland from Salvador), is the gateway to the magical 'Diamond Mountain' national park. The extraordinary landscape is made up of bizarre rock formations, caves, waterfalls and subterranean rivers. Here, in the 18th century, an enormous vein of diamonds was discovered, prompting a rush of prospectors, known as *garimpeiros*, whose trails are now followed by walkers.

The best way to explore the park is by foot, bike or horse. Those who want to take to the water can swim in waterholes or hire canoes.

Only 30 minutes' pretty walk west of Lençóis, **Ribeirao do Meio** is a rock-slide with a 30-m (100-ft) waterfall.

At 340m (1,115ft), the **Cachoeira da Fumaça** is a rather larger cascade. It is named after the mist (or 'smoke') created by the tumbling falls, which are thought to be the highest in Brazil.

Underground caverns are a haven for divers and caving enthusiasts, but access must be granted by environmental protection agencies. **Gruta da Pratinha** is reached by a 'staircase' that descends into a crystal-clear lake, while the near 'impossible' entrance of **Os Impossíveis** leads to a 35-m (115-ft) pit of tunnels and white stalagmites. Rappelling is possible down many of the cliff faces and into waterfall and caves, such as **Gruta de Lapão**, a rare sandstone and quartzite cave stretching for more than 1km (2/3 mile). And various hills (*morros*), such as the 1,170-m (3,838-ft) high Morro do Pai Inácio, can be scaled.

Jericoacoara

This remote area of spectacular beaches, enormous dunes, coconut trees, reefs and lagoons was once little more than an isolated fishing village in the northeast. Although its idyllic reputation is still deserved and it remains a real journey to get to, 'Jeri', as it is known, has become very popular, particularly with young travellers. Be prepared for a long, rough ride from Fortaleza that will take the best part of a day, and for an absence of roads when you finally arrive.

Most visitors are content with 'chilling out' and listening to the stories and poems of the wise old local fishermen. For others, there is hiking, windsurfing on **Jijoca Lake** and horse and dune buggy riding. Accommodation was once just in hammocks and simple lodges, but there

Strolling and sailing – Jericoacoara provides a serene scene

are increasing numbers of hotels with pools. Electricity came in 1998, but street illumination is forbidden, so there is just the light of the moon to show you your way at night. 'Nightlife' consists of sitting on the **Duna do por do Sol** (Sunset Dune) to watch the sun fall into the sea, and perhaps an evening of the traditional local music and dance, *forró*.

Jericoacoara – an indigenous word meaning 'hole of the turtles' – is now part of an Environmental Protection Area. Walking is the most environmentally friendly activity you can undertake, but there are also excursions available: jeep rides to **Tatajuba**, a village 25km (15$^1/_2$ miles) west that has disappeared under the dunes, and to **Mangue Seco**, another lovely beach, or ferry rides across the **Guriú** river.

Caruaru is justly famed for its clay handicrafts

The sertão

This hot, semi-arid region of 'drylands' covers three quarters of northeastern Brazil. Characterised by *caatinga* (named after its scrub-like shrub) and cacti, the land here is peopled by inhabitants who barely scrape a living from the dusty earth. Although this is a poor region with few obvious sights and few visitors, the *sertão* has been the inspiration for some of the country's greatest literature, poetry and music, and continues to loom large in the Brazilian imagination.

The ghosts of the now flooded town of **Canudos** (*see 'History', p11*) are here, as well as the tales of the old men and women who have lived so hard and so long. **Triungo** is a lovely village with cobbled streets surrounded by waterfalls; **Piranhas** is another, with multicoloured houses, on the banks of the River São Francisco.

Caruaru, 135km (84 miles) from Recife, is recognised around the world for its clay handicrafts. Feira Livre is a great, twice-weekly event with musicians, food and artisans and is very popular with tourists. Feira de Caruaru is the town's daily 'fair', the largest local market in the northeast, selling fresh produce as well as electronics and handicrafts. Hawkers sell copies of popular poems hung from string, *literatura do cordel* (literally 'string literature').

Alto de Moura, 6km (3$^3/_4$ miles) west of Caruaru, is a community of potters producing *figurinhas* (clay figures). Most

Cool down in Chapada dos Guimarães

of them are descendants of the 'master' Mestre Vitalino, whose workshops on the main (and only) street of the same name are open to visitors.

Parque Nacional da Chapada dos Guimarães

This peaceful national park 65km (40 miles) north of Cuiabá can be conveniently combined with a visit to the Pantanal. The dramatic canyons and plateaux sculpted from red rock sandstone are reminiscent of the American Midwest, yet also feature clear waterfalls and pristine forests. In the centre of Brazil, a *mirante* (lookout) just outside the national park is the unofficial geographic centre of South America.

Tours are easily arranged to this geologically and ecologically interesting region full of bird life, which usually combine walking with four-wheel driving. The park has few tourist facilities, and trails are badly signposted and poorly maintained. On top of that, there is a danger of snakes, so a guide is essential. Avoid visiting at weekends when the park becomes crowded with Brazilian tourists.

A popular, half-day trip takes in the seven waterfalls of the **Sete de Setembro** river and the **'House of Rock'**, a small sandstone cave sculpted by its waters. **Véu de Noiva** (Bridal Veil) is just one of the many falls where it is possible to swim; for the best view, walk to see it from below, but take a guide. The **Cidade de Pedra** (City of Stone) is a cluster of unusual rock formations created by the elements; it lies 20km ($12^1/_2$ miles) north of the town of Chapada. For those who want to really work up a sweat, the difficult hike to the top of the mountain **São Jerônimo** (1,020m/3,346ft) is rewarded by spectacular panoramic views of the surrounding national park.

When to go

In Brazil, the seasons are the reverse of those in Europe and the US. Summer is from December to February, when sunshine and Carnaval make it a very popular 'winter' destination for travellers escaping the cold of home. This is also when most Brazilians take their holiday, so accommodation and flights are more expensive, bookings are harder to get and the beaches in particular are more crowded. The ideal time to travel is October to November and March to April when the weather is not too hot and the hordes have gone home.

If you're on a budget, Carnaval is perhaps the time *not* to go. Prices of accommodation quadruple and the cost of flights, tours and taxis goes through the roof; consider visiting in the run-up to enjoy the build-up and rehearsals (*see 'Carnaval', pp94–5*).

Climate

Brazil is almost the size of Western Europe, with variations in climate to match. The northern parts of the country are the hottest, the southern the coldest, where frosts and below-freezing temperatures are not uncommon. That said, the country is tropical or subtropical and humid almost all over, and during the summer months it can get uncomfortably hot wherever you are. Heat in the Amazon, however, is something of a myth; temperatures rarely reach more than 32°C (90°F), with little seasonal variation. The northeast is the hottest part of the country, where temperatures regularly reach more than 38°C (100°F).

Rain can fall at any time, but it is generally short-lived and welcome, with the rainy season occurring during the

Extremes of climate are a fact of life here

summer months. The Amazon is one of the wettest places on earth and moist year-round. The interior of Brazil, particularly in the northeast, is so arid that droughts regularly cause large numbers of deaths.

RIO DE JANEIRO

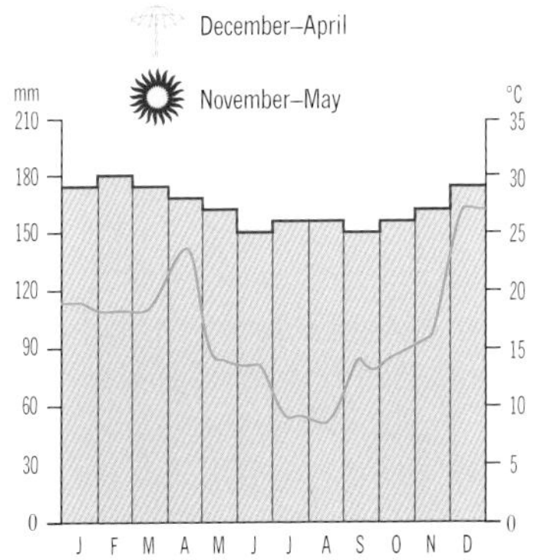

SALVADOR

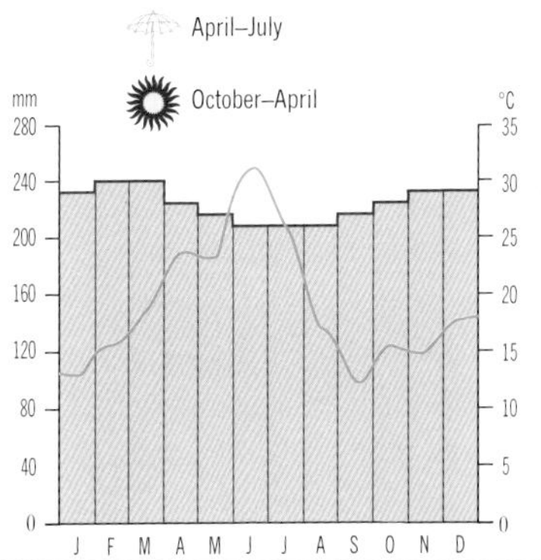

WEATHER CONVERSION CHART

25.4mm = 1 inch

°F = 1.8 × °C + 32

FLORIANÓPOLIS

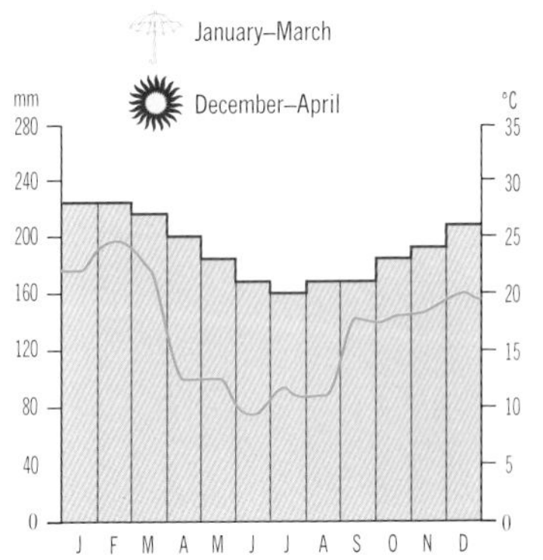

MANAUS

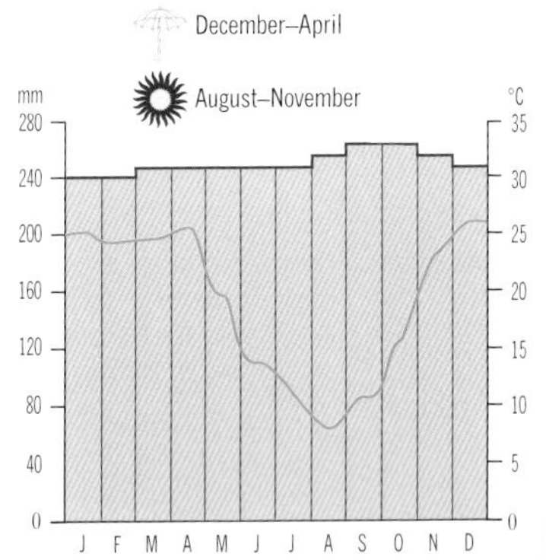

FORTALEZA

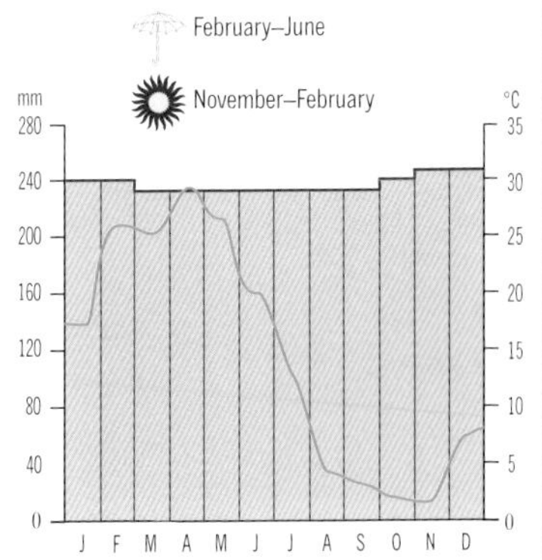

Getting around

Brazil is more than 4,000km (2,485 miles) from east to west and about the same from north to south – the distance from London to Baghdad. Travel within the country is not the headache it might be, thanks to a decent network of long-distance buses (except in the Amazon where riverboats are the main form of transport). There is a well-developed airline system, with several budget companies competing with the large scheduled carriers to many destinations, although industrial action regularly causes delays.

By bus

A good deal cheaper than air travel, buses come in three flavours. *Convencional* or *comum* is the basic intercity service, with an onboard toilet. 'Golden' or *executivio* vehicles are generally air-conditioned with reclining chairs, onboard video and a bit more legroom. And *Leito* are sleeper buses with seats to rival business class on an aircraft, complete with personal audio systems so those who want to sleep don't have to listen to the video soundtrack; you will usually be given basic snacks, water and coffee, a pillow and a blanket.

Brazil is well supplied with airlines

Two of the biggest companies offering the full complement of services are **Itapemirim** (*www.itapemirim.com.br*) and **Auto Viação 1001** (*www.autoviacao1001.com.br*). Although their websites are in Portuguese, it is fairly easy to check services, times and costs online. Buy tickets at the bus station at least a day in advance. When making a reservation, avoid seats over the wheelbase or near the toilets. Those who don't book may find themselves standing in the aisles – not a pleasant prospect on a long journey.

By train

For decades, Brazil's railways had been haemorrhaging money, and there is now no real passenger network to speak of. There are, however, some fairly short leisure routes that have been kept going, or restored for tourists. The weekend train ride from Angra dos Reis up to Lidice is a scenic 40-km (25-mile) journey through the Atlantic forest (*see 'Angra dos Reis', p48*). An historic 1940s steam train (*www.tremdavale.com.br*) runs between Mariana and Ouro Preto (20km/12½ miles), and another, from 1912, runs further south on the old gold trail between São João del Rei and Tiradentes (12km/7½ miles). Both these services operate twice daily.

By air

Brazil's airline industry has been in the midst of something of a crisis since a passenger airliner collided with a small private jet over the Amazon in 2006. All 154 people aboard the larger plane were killed in Brazil's worst ever air disaster. The crash has brought to light 'black holes' in radar coverage over the Amazon, among a plethora of other problems with Brazil's undefended air traffic control system. Since then a

BRAZILIAN AIRLINES

Gol	*Tel: (11) 2125 3200. www.voegol.com.br*
OceanAir	*Tel: (11/21) 4004 4040. www.oceanair.com.br*
Rico	*Tel: (92) 4009 8333. www.voerico.com.br*
TAM	*Tel: (11/21) 4002 5700. www.tam.com.br*
Trip	*Tel: (19) 3139 3100. www.airtrip.com.br*
Varig	*Tel: (11/21) 4003 7000. www.varig.com.br*

Santa Teresa's historic tramline

number of strikes, work-to-rules and go-slows have caused misery at airports.

The national airline, Varig, went bust in 2006 and has recently been snapped up by budget airline Gol whose plane it was that crashed over the Amazon. Gol's aim is to keep Varig going as a separate entity, while attempting to find operational savings. Most airlines have websites, but often you will be unable to purchase a ticket online with a non-Brazilian credit card, so be prepared for a trip to the travel agents.

When it comes to reaching the Amazon, air travel is the only option for those without the time for a lengthy coastal voyage. Flight costs have come down but routes can be tortuous, often involving transfer via hubs like São Paulo and Brasilia. Once at a jungle hub (Manaus or Belém), travellers often have the option of an air taxi on to the more remote jungle lodges, but river transport is a cheaper and more environmentally friendly option.

By boat

From Belém on the Amazonian coast there are regular ferries upriver to destinations such as Santarém and Manaus. In many cases, it is possible to hire a hammock for the duration of the trip, with meals taken on board. Allow four to seven days for a trip to Manaus, a day or two less if you are travelling downstream from Manaus. Upgrading to a cabin is a possibility on many boats; although the price rises steeply for this option, it is highly recommended. These days, with airline costs coming down, the river trip to Manaus is not quite the bargain it was, but it is still a unique experience. Many such trips can be booked from home, but you will typically get a better deal if you are prepared to negotiate in Belém.

In the Amazon, rivers are the main roads

Timetables

For up-to-date details of bus, ferry and train services, consult the Thomas Cook *Overseas Timetable*, published bi-monthly, available to buy online at *www.thomascookpublishing.com, tel: 01733 416477* or from branches of Thomas Cook in the UK.

By car

Driving in Brazil's big cities can be a hair-raising experience, even though these days more drivers take account of the traffic lights. In the countryside, away from the main coastal highways, road conditions vary enormously from fairly decent to unbelievably bad. Main national highways are numbered and prefixed 'BR', with smaller roads prefixed with state codes. All traffic drives on the right, seat belts are compulsory, and drivers must be at least 18, but generally over 21 to hire a car.

By taxi

In big cities, cheap taxis are easy to find on the street. You will often be charged a premium from outside a large hotel. Check the meter is working before you set off; if travelling a long distance, it may be cheaper to negotiate an off-meter price beforehand, but ensure the deal is clearly understood. Watch out for unscrupulous drivers and money scams, particularly at the airports and late at night.

Access for travellers with disabilities

Brazil is not particularly well set up for travellers with disabilities, and getting around can be problematic, particularly if your visit is unaccompanied. With 15 per cent of Brazilians suffering a disability that limits use of transport, Brazil is slowly waking up to its responsibilities, but almost all 'public' transport is privately owned and, so far, investment in accessible buses, not to mention urban design, has been inadequate. Bus travel is practically impossible without help, and taxis are difficult. However, many tour operators run custom-designed tours, and even travel to the Amazon, though challenging, is possible.

A thrilling boat ride into the rushing Iguaçu Falls

Accommodation

The old estate agent's adage 'Location, location, location' is key to choosing where to stay in Brazil, where distances are huge and built-up areas change in character very quickly. The difference between even neighbouring Copacabana and Ipanema in Rio is significant in everything from atmosphere to price, and the same goes for all the cities. There are huge regional variations as well of course, so that the south has a large number of sophisticated business hotels, for example, while accommodation in the Pantanal and Amazon is by its very nature rustic, with intermittent water and plenty of bugs. 'Eco hotels' are often no such thing.

Booking

Book ahead during the peak summer holiday period from December to February and of course during Carnaval. If you are doing a large amount of independent travelling and have a decent understanding of Portuguese, consider buying the highly respected *Guia do Brasil Quatro Rodas* from any newsstand. Updated every year, it not only features excellent hotel and restaurant reviews but also has detailed maps.

Star quality

The old star rating system does not reflect factors such as quality of service, and many superb hotels are unrated. If you are using it as a basis for choosing a hotel, go at least one star higher than you would normally, to avoid disappointment; ratings here do not correspond to international standards. Luxury accommodation is often disappointing, particularly in terms of service and décor. Owner-run establishments have been featured wherever possible in this guide, and offer some of the best accommodation in Brazil.

What's in a name?

Pousadas are small, often family-run, hotels, the best of which are on a par

The Copacabana Palace hotel in Rio

Pousadas offer intimate charm for all budgets

with boutique hotels. In rural areas *fazendas* (ranches) have opened their doors to tourism, while lodges in the Amazon and Pantanal have been purpose-built for visitors. In these remote areas, accommodation is usually offered on an all-inclusive basis, with tours and all food part of the package. Apartments (*temporada* or *apartamentos para aluguel*) are a good option in cities, even for stays of just a few days, representing very good value, especially if you are in a group, and the freedom to cook and come and go as you please – particularly valuable if you are travelling with children. Note that rooms with bathrooms are called *apartamentos*, those without a bathroom *quartos*, and that a 'bathroom' will usually just include a shower. *Motéis* are 'love' motels and rented by the hour.

Charm and luxury

Members of the independent hotel association Roteiros de Charme (*www.roteirosdecharme.com.br*) have been featured wherever possible in this guide. Invariably excellent, with great locations and service and a commitment to sustainable tourism, they are often in historic buildings, traditional farms, centuries-old mansions and country houses.

Bed on a budget

The Camping Clube do Brasil (*www.campingclube.com.br, Portuguese only*) has more than 50 sites throughout the country. If you choose not to camp on an official site, make sure to cause as little impact on the environment as possible. There are nearly 100 *albergues de juventude* (youth hostels, *www.hostel.org.br*), some of which have rooms in addition to *dormitórios* (dormitories), as well as regular hostels. Cama e Café (*www.camaecafe.com.br*) is an innovative enterprise offering 'bed and breakfast' in family houses in Rio's Santa Teresa.

Food and drink

Eating in Brazil is a joy. Tender beef dried in the sun, exotic Amazonian fruit, jewel-like sushi, and rich African seafood stew are all 'national' dishes. You don't need to physically travel throughout the country to get a taste of Brazil's delicious diversity; just tuck in.

Brazil in a mouthful

The Amazon's mouthwatering freshwater fish and juice-filled fruits found nowhere else in the world are part of the native Indian cuisine that has been snapped up by some of Brazil's finest chefs. *Churrasco* (barbecue) and *carne do sol* (sun-dried meat) may have originated with the cowboys and muleteers from the centre and the south, but they're now served in some of the country's best restaurants. Manioc, also called cassava, was first cultivated by the indigenous people around 4,000 years ago. The calorific root remains a staple in the impoverished north, and *farofa* (coarsely roasted manioc flour) is used as a condiment as common as salt.

Beans means...

Feijoada is a stew of black bean, pork trimmings, sausages, ribs and dried beef that is not so much a dish as a ritual. Eaten for Saturday lunch and on special occasions, its very preparation is a celebration. The story goes that slaves used every bit of the pig, including its snout, ears and tail – leftovers from the masters' table. In poorer parts of the country, many people survive on a diet consisting almost exclusively of *arroz e feijão* (beans and rice). *Caldo de feijão* is a filling bean soup often served in a glass as an appetiser or downed before a drinking session.

A taste of home

Almost five million African slaves were shipped to Brazil. They brought their recipes with them, introducing *dendê* (palm) oil, chilli peppers and coconut milk to their new home. *Moqueca*, a rich stew of prawns, white fish, tomatoes and chilli, is the classic Afro-Brazilian dish. In the 20th century, the Portuguese settlers were followed by Italian and German immigrants, followed by Syrians, Lebanese and Japanese. They have all left a rich imprint; sushi in Brazil is superlative, pizza and pasta are ubiquitous, and

Arabic staples such as *kibe* or couscous provide healthy fast-food options.

Fast food

Pop into any *lanchonete* (café) or *padaria* (bakery) for a *salgadinho* (small snack) such as a *pão de queijo* (cheese bread) or an *empadinha* (small pasty). An *X-tudo* is a hamburger with all the trimmings, a *misto quente* a toasted ham and cheese sandwich. *Petiscos* are bar snacks that can be meals in themselves – don't miss melt-in-the-mouth *bolinhos de bacalhau* (codfish balls). For a quick feed, *comida a kilo* (food by weight) cannot be beaten for choice and cost.

The most important meal of the day

Café da manhã (breakfast) for most Brazilians is *café com leite* (hot milk coffee) with some bread and jam and maybe ham or cheese. Most hotels will also serve a selection of fresh fruit, cereals and sometimes eggs as part of a buffet included in the room price.

Going green

Pizza, salad, beans and *acompanhamentos* (side dishes) of vegetables will be the base meals for vegetarians in Brazil. In restaurants ask for items '*sem carne*' (without meat) and make sure that beans and soups

Fresh fish on sale in Manaus

have not been made with meat stock. A *restaurante natural* will offer a range of vegetarian and soya dishes. Don't dismiss *churrascurias* (steak houses) which usually have good salad bars.

Menu decoder A to Z

abacate	avocado
alface	lettuce
alho	garlic
arroz	white rice
atúm	tuna
bacalhau	cod
batata	potato
bife	steak
camarão	prawn
carne	meat
cenoura	carrot
coco	coconut
frango	chicken
fruto	fruit
langosta	lobster
limão	lime
mariscos	seafood
ovos	eggs
pão	bread
peixe	fish
peru	turkey
porco	pork
presunto	ham
queijo	cheese
siri	crab
sobremesa	dessert
verduras	vegetables

Fresh snacks soak up the beer

Drink to Brazil

A whole range of juices (*sucos*) made with exotic fruits is available, many unknown outside the country's borders. *Água de coco* (coconut water) is delicious and great for rehydrating on a hot day or after too many cocktails. Coffee is, of course, big in Brazil, although many of the better beans are exported. Brazilians drink *cafezinhos* (literally 'little coffees') throughout the day; the question '*Você toma um cafezinho?*' ('Do you want a coffee?') is a social nicety akin to a handshake.

There are no licensing laws in Brazil, so you can get something to drink day or night. Brazilian bottled beer (*cerveja*) is particularly good. Antarctica is a popular brand sold throughout the country. Draught beer is called *chopp*. National wine (*vinho*) is generally

EATING ETIQUETTE

In smarter restaurants a *couvert* (appetiser) is often served; if you don't want to be charged for it, just politely send it back. Portions are often for two to share; if you find you have ordered too much, ask for the remainder '*para levar*' (to take away) and give it to someone on the street – it won't take long to find a happy recipient. In the northeast, lunch is the main meal of the day and dinner a light snack. In the south, people don't go out to dinner *before* 10pm.

pretty undrinkable; go for Chilean or Argentinian bottles instead. *Cachaça*, the local firewater (white rum made from sugar cane), is combined with fresh fruit juice to make delicious and dangerous *batidas*. *Cachaça* mixed with sugar, crushed ice and limes makes a *caipirinha*, the sublime Brazilian cocktail.

Tip top

Try to tip at least 15 per cent. If possible, leave the money in cash rather than putting it on your credit card to avoid it going straight into the owner's pocket. Waiting staff are paid next to nothing in Brazil and rely heavily on tips just to survive. The price of a chocolate bar could feed a whole hungry family in Brazil.

A coffee plantation in Minas Gerais

Entertainment

When it comes to having a good time, you are unlikely to be short of options in Brazil. If anything, you will run out of time or energy long before you run out of things to do and people to see. Don't be afraid to start up a conversation; Brazilians are very open and make friends easily. However, don't be too offended if they show up late or not at all. If you don't speak Portuguese, most Brazilians understand some Spanish, and in Rio and São Paulo, a good few speak English.

Carnaval

Of course, the highlight of the entertainment year is Carnaval (*see pp94–95*), an extravaganza like no other, whether it's the street parties in Salvador or Rio's ticket-only Sambódromo. If you are visiting during Carnaval, your hotel will probably arrange tickets for you. If you wait till you get here, you are likely to be disappointed, or find yourself in the hands of a tout demanding a ridiculous price. In the run-up to Rio's Carnaval, it is possible to participate in (or at least watch) the samba school rehearsals, which are held in the Sambódromo in the preceding weeks. There are no elaborate costumes, but the grandstands are full and the atmosphere is almost as electrifying as the real thing.

In Salvador, those who are a little wary of the chaos on the streets might consider signing up with a *bloco* (Carnaval group) for the evening. Identified by your *bloco* 'uniform', you are then allowed within the protected area of that group as it makes its way through the streets, and you'll have access to their support truck with bar and toilets.

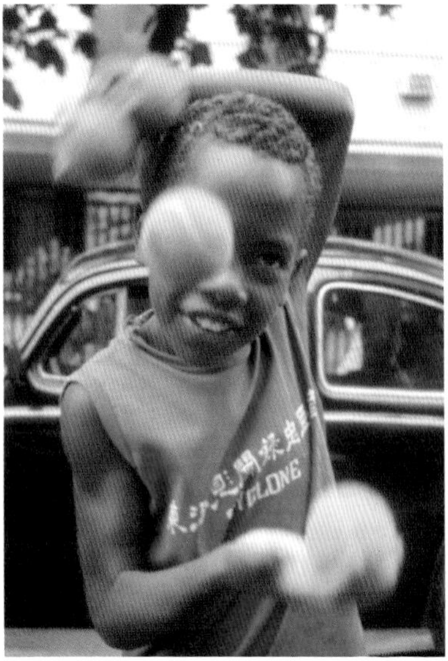

Entertainment on every street corner

Cookery courses

The distinctive cuisine of Brazil's chief culinary regions, the Amazon, Minas Gerais and Bahia, is best embraced with some 'hands-on' lessons. Courses usually include gourmet meals in nearby restaurants, with market visits and trips to sugar and coffee plantations sometimes added. Programmes can often be combined with a Portuguese language course and cultural visits; most courses will at least touch on Brazil's cuisine in relation to its cultural history. The commercial, somewhat Americanised **Academy of Cooking and Other Pleasures** (*www.chefbrazil.com*) runs five-day programmes in Paraty and Ouro Preto.

Eating out

A night at a *rodízio churrascaria* (literally 'a rotation barbecue') is an event in itself, a unique Brazilian experience that is not to be missed. These are all-you-can-eat steakhouses showcasing the finest in Brazilian beef. A succession of waiters brings different cuts to your table, their offerings accompanied by a buffet with a huge variety of salads and often seafood too. These are lively, noisy places, and great fun.

Gay life

Rio is Brazil's gay capital, where there are plenty of clubs for gay men and women and even a gay part of the beach, opposite Rua Farme de Amoedo (*www.riogayguide.com*). São Paulo, if anything even more cosmopolitan, is home to probably the world's largest gay pride festival, which takes place every year, usually in June. Outside the main cities gay entertainment – when it exists at all – is more underground.

Carnaval at Pátio de São Pedro square in Recife

High culture

Unless you understand Portuguese, a night of live drama may be too demanding, but ballet, opera and orchestral recitals are a different matter. The CCBB (*see p37*) and the Theatro Municipal (*Praça Floriano. Tel: (21) 2262 3935. www.theatromunicipal.rj.gov.br*) are Rio's top cultural venues. São Paulo has its own municipal theatre (*Praça Ramos de Azevedo. Tel: (11) 3222 8698*) dating from 1911, and even the Amazon has grand opera houses in Belém (*see p114*) and Manaus (*see p117*). For a complete list of events in all cities consult the online guide, Viva Música (*www.vivamusica.com.br*).

Nightlife

Music (*see 'Culture', p16*) and dance are never off the menu in Brazilian bars and clubs, although the liveliest nights are Thursday to Saturday. Live music from the local *forró* to more international jazz is easy to come by in bars, often without a cover charge. Street musicians work hard for tips outside tourist restaurants; try to give them some change. The locals like to go out late, particularly at the weekends when things do not really get going until 10 or 11pm. In Rio and São Paulo, the nightlife scene is incredibly fluid, but there are plenty of free guides around (e.g. the *Nomad Guide*) to let you know what is happening. These can usually be found in the lobbies of upmarket hotels, or in bars and restaurants. Both cities attract big-name DJs and live acts of international calibre. Buzzing, bustling street parties spring up outside clubs and bars, fuelled by ramshackle stands selling beers and *caipirinhas*. If the weather is fine, these attract hundreds of revellers well into the small hours.

Street stalls mix cocktails at any hour

STREET BARS

Rodas de Samba (literally 'wheels of Samba') are mobile groups of street musicians who wander between Rio's street bars on weekends and holidays. These street bars are typically full of customers, weekends or not, and offer the musicians a captive audience. The concept of a street bar is not unique, but in Rio they are found on almost every corner, their patrons with their backs to the world, sipping beer, placing bets, watching football and discussing the ills of the world. Though never the most salubrious of establishments, these are fun places to cool down with a beer or two.

For the kids

Most parents know that their enjoyment of a holiday depends on whether the children can be kept entertained (*see 'Children', pp152–3*). Most large hotels have televisions showing some English programmes, although you would be well advised to bring a stack of DVDs to entertain your offspring in emergencies, and during long journeys. Some hotels geared to children have a range of facilities, from games rooms to kids' clubs and even babysitters. **Superclubs** in Bahia (*www.superclubs.com*) has an extraordinary programme of all-inclusive entertainment for both children and adults, though it can all feel a little manufactured. Some of the newer airports even have a *berçário* (nursery) where your children can play and even be bathed.

Rodas de Samba musicians wander from bar to bar

Shopping

*The arts and crafts of Brazil are exceptional. In particular, the rich folkloric craft tradition in the northeast produces sought-after ceramics, painted clay figures and woodcarvings. Don't miss Caruaru (*see 'Getting away from it all', p128*), a day trip from Recife, if you are in the area.*

A little piece of Brazil

There is no end of tempting souvenirs, from unique Brazilian hammocks to fashionable clothing and percussion instruments. The *berimbau* that forms the backing track to the fighting/dancing art form Capoeira may be impractical to take home, but there are many smaller options, such as tambourines, small drums or the *cavaquinho*, a Brazilian version of the ukulele. Music CDs are a good choice and generally of good quality, prompting endless memories and taking up little space in a suitcase.

Wooden handicrafts take many forms

Soapstone trinkets are very cheap but may not last the journey home. You can't go wrong with Haivanas, light, funky flip-flops featuring the Brazilian flag and costing a fraction of what they do at home. Still a fashion accessory after all these years, they are eminently practical and suitable for everyone from children to ravers.

The national football kit is another winner and available in all sizes. Brazil is known for leather goods such as shoes, belts, wallets and luggage, but although they may be durable they are not always of the best quality. Underwear is attractive and cheap, but the tiny bikinis may well be too revealing to wear at home.

Markets and malls

Some of the best places to shop in Brazil are its markets. Salvador has the

Mercado Modelo, there's the hippy market in Ipanema, the former prisons of Recife and Natal are now filled with craft stalls, and Belém has its witches' market. Locals prefer to shop in 'state-of-the-art' American-style shopping malls, known as 'shoppings'. Although some may find them bland, these outlets have the advantage of cool air-conditioning and offer everything under one roof. Shopping malls also open late – until around 10pm – and on Sundays, so it is easy to fit shopping trips around beach visits and sightseeing. Rio's **Botafogo Praia Shopping** even has an open-air bar and food-court with a close-up of Sugarloaf, as well as a cinema. In malls and elsewhere, *Livrarias* (bookshops) are often a joy, where punters can peruse books and magazines for free while enjoying a coffee.

Works of art

The Amazonian Indians create outstanding pieces made of clay, wood and even bark and seeds, with many of the crafts specific to certain tribes. And lace-makers in the south continue a European trend brought over by the Portuguese in the 16th century.

Buying smart

No one wants to buy objects plundered from the jungle, and restrictions apply to certain goods, such as those made from some skins and seeds. **FUNAI Fundação Nacional do Índio** (National Foundation for Indians) is a government agency that protects national Indian interests and culture, with shops all over Brazil.

Paying for it

Markets, and even many shops, only accept cash. Brazil's international airports are unusual in that they offer duty-free shopping facilities on arrival, although by law shops cannot accept local currency.

Every day is market day in Manaus

Sport and leisure

Brazilians embrace the active life; they love to be outdoors, and like to keep fit. Blessed as they are with 7,500km (4,660 miles) of coastline, it is no surprise that many activities revolve around the beach, surf and sea, but there are plenty of choices away from the coast too.

Cycling

For those who like to get around on two wheels, Brazil can be a challenge. Traffic accidents are depressingly common and the injured parties are very often those who have been knocked from their bikes. In São Paulo, the 3-km (2-mile) flyover known as the Minhocão (Big Worm) is closed to cars on Sundays and attracts cyclists who use the day to meet up with friends for a bit of exercise, interspersed with visits to bakeries, ice-cream shops and bars along the route. Alongside Rio's beach, there is a cycle lane open all week, which expands to four lanes on Sundays, when traffic is banned from the adjacent road.

Diving and snorkelling

Brazil's Costa Verde (Green Coast) is overflowing with fantastic dive sites, with opportunities for coral dives and exploration of sunken wrecks just two of the highlights (*see 'Sunken treasure', p54*). Head to Ilha Grande (*see 'Ilha Grande', p50*) or Angra dos Reis (*see 'Angra dos Reis', p48*) and book a dive excursion there, rather than in Rio or from home, where the price is likely to be higher.

For those heading further south, the coastal waters of Santa Catarina are another hot spot, particularly the Bombinhas peninsula (*see 'Florianópolis and Santa Catarina', p62*) with its superb visibility and protected sea life. Always check that instructors are PADI certified, and ask around in port about the quality of tours before you commit. If your Portuguese is limited, it is advisable to seek out an English-speaking instructor/guide.

Fishing

The rich waters of the Amazon are teeming with countless varieties of tasty freshwater fish, and many lodges organise atmospheric fishing expeditions using traditional canoes (*see 'Into the jungle', p118*). The Pantanal, too, is filled with freshwater delights, but for those who prefer sea fishing, Paraty and Ilha Grande are good bets.

Fishing tackle can be purchased or hired in Paraty and Ilha Grande, but for the Pantanal you need to take your equipment with you or have it provided by your tour guide.

Football

Brazilian football is renowned the world over and it is by far the nation's favourite sport; however, the game itself is not in a good state. Close to 1,000 of the best players are transferred abroad every year as clubs struggle to survive in a fiercely competitive environment. There are almost too many players and too many decaying white-elephant stadiums spread too thinly across the country, making average attendances in Brazil the lowest of any country in South America.

The up-side is that it is easy to get a ticket to almost any game. International operators such as Fanfare (*www.fanfare-events.com*) list upcoming fixtures and will organise your trip to the game, as will most large hotels. It is, of course, much cheaper to buy a ticket direct from the stadium. For those used to the rough and tumble of football matches at home, this is probably the best option; still, you should aim for a

Cycling is popular, especially on Sundays

seat away from the madness at the top of the terraces. If you are worried about getting home safely from the game, go with a tour.

WORLD CUP 2014

When Colombia dropped out of the running, Brazil became the only nation bidding to host the 2014 World Cup. However, the country does not have a single venue that meets international standards, and Lula, Brazil's president, admitted that the country would have to build at least 12 new stadiums for the competition. Many believe that staging a football tournament, in light of Brazil's massive foreign debt and grinding poverty, should be the last of the country's priorities, though if Brazil wins, most people will almost certainly find themselves in agreement with the decision.

Hiking and trekking

Rio's Tijuca forest is made for nature-lovers (*see 'Green Rio', p40*) and is just a stone's throw from the city centre. For those who want to spend days or weeks in the wilderness, a trip to the Pantanal (*see p74*) is a good choice, more so than the Amazon where the dense jungle inhibits sightings of wildlife.

If you are planning on doing a decent amount of hiking, take precautions against extremes of weather, and always make sure someone responsible knows where you have gone and when to expect you back.

Horse riding in the Pantanal

Horse riding and racing

The Pantanal, with its sometimes marshy lands, is perfect for horseback excursions. Visitors can keep their feet dry and spot the wildlife on the plains from an elevated viewpoint, and horses are able to take routes that are even beyond 4WD vehicles. The steep climbs on the Estrada Real in Minas Gerais (*see 'Head for the hills', p72*) provide another prime opportunity to take to the saddle.

For those who would rather watch than take part, head to the Hipódromo da Gávea, home to Rio's Jockey Club (*www.jcb.com.br*). Sandwiched between the Botanic Gardens and the lake, and with views of Sugarloaf, it is one of the world's most spectacular racecourses.

Surfing

The wild ocean-facing side of Ilha Santa Catarina (*see 'Florianópolis and Santa Catarina', p62*) is perfect for surfers who want to escape the crowds of Rio's surfing beaches (*see 'Active Rio', p42*). Windsurfing is growing in popularity here, and even kite-surfing is beginning to capture the imagination of the locals. At present, the availability of equipment is probably holding back these two sports, but head to Búzios (*see p44*) or Fortaleza (*see p108*) and you will more than likely find a few like-minded souls with wind in their sails.

Yoga, massage and spas

All manner of keep-fit fanatics head to Rio's city beaches, but you don't have to be a body-builder or professional footballer to join in. In Ipanema, beach yoga classes are a great way to relax, and there are a number of massage stations where you can soak up the sun while getting a professional high-quality treatment. There are also morning yoga classes in Rio's botanic gardens (*see 'Green Rio', p40*), and dedicated yoga and spa holidays have taken off here in recent years, notably in beach resorts like Paraty. By contrast, Caxambu is an old-school mineral spa resort, a small town that is 300km (186 miles) from Rio in the state of Minas Gerais.

Adrenaline sports of all kinds are on offer

Children

There is no reason why your children should not have as much fun as you in Brazil – if not more. The easy-going Brazilians warm quickly to visitors of all ages and are very tolerant, if not downright welcoming, towards children everywhere from restaurants to museums. Of course, the huge distances, both internationally and internally, the language and general exoticism will challenge even the most hardened of travellers with children, but the rewards are huge and everyone can learn from the Brazilians who always seem to smile whatever the circumstances.

City limits

Rio's **Museu do Índio** (*www.museudoindio.org.br*) is one of the most important Indian museums in Latin America. Children can paint themselves with indigenous designs and explore models of native houses.

The award-winning **Estação Ciência** (*www.eciencia.usp.br*) in São Paulo is a science station with lots of interactive exhibits and an education area for Brazilian children from troubled backgrounds.

São Paulo's **Instituto Butantan** (Snake Farm, *www.butantan.gov.br*) is another fascinating destination for kids, with a large collection of poisonous snakes and an open-air pit.

Clean fun

Baixo Bebe in Rio's Leblon is a wonderful beach spot where babies and small children can play while parents socialise the *carioca* way. There are toys, a nappy changing area, and when the tide recedes, the sand bank creates paddling pools for little ones.

Most families will be content with the beach, but for protected swimming and some thrills, there are **water parks** up and down the country. There are **Wet'n'Wild** water parks on the outskirts of Rio, Salvador and São Paulo (*www.wetnwild.com.br/wet*), 20km (12½ miles) from Recife is **Veneza Water Park** (*www.venezawaterpark.com.br*), and **Beach Park** (*www.beachpark.com.br*) near Fortaleza is one of the largest in Latin America.

Feeding time

Pão de queijo (cheese bread) and thick-crust pizza can be had on every street corner. Older children may revel in the chance to eat crocodile steaks with French fries in the Pantanal, and *churrasco* (barbecue meat) – traditional cowboy fare. Guaraná is Brazil's answer to Coca-Cola, a fizzy drink made from an Amazonian berry. Don't miss the delicious *água de coco* (coconut milk) and the huge variety of *sucos* (fresh juices) made with everything from *maracujá* (passion fruit) to *açaí*, an exotic Brazilian fruit. For a fruit milkshake, ask for a *vitamina*.

Learning curve

Some of the poorest children in the world live in Brazil, where there are eight million street children alone. **SOS Children's Villages** (*www.soschildrensvillages.org.uk*) offers the chance to sponsor an orphaned or abandoned Brazilian child.

The **Didá** music school for disadvantaged girls (*see 'Salvador (cidade alta)', p84*) and **Friends of Maria** (*www.friendsofmaria.com*) for homeless children in Salvador are just two other inspiring social projects, both of which welcome donations and visitors.

And a glimpse of life in a *favela* anywhere in the country (*see 'A girl from the favela', p38*) is an enlightening and uplifting experience.

The wild life

Come face to face with big-toothed caiman, watch cheeky monkeys, and fish for piranha in the **Amazon** or the **Pantanal**. Wildlife-watching excursions in these areas involve thrilling canoe trips and open-top jeep safaris which kids absolutely love.

And for thrill-seeking youngsters, you can't beat riding high on towering **sand dunes** in the northeast (*see 'Dune buggy adventure', p110*) or taking the plunge in a boat to the edge of **Iguaçu** waterfalls (*see p65*); there's rafting and tree climbing in the national park as well.

There is plenty to explore at the beach

Essentials

Arriving

Rio's international airport is Galeão – Antonio Carlos Jobim (GIG). Rio is 11 hours by air from London, though most flights are routed via São Paulo, adding an hour to the journey. From LA, Rio is 14 hours via Miami, from New York, 12 hours direct. From Sydney it is 21, from Cape Town 15, and from Auckland 17, all via Buenos Aires. Travellers from Europe should be wary of cheap flight deals via the US that involve passing through US customs and are prone to the seemingly endemic delays of American carriers. Allow 40 minutes to get into town from the airport – more during rush hour – and always take a licensed taxi.

Customs

The following items are exempt from duty on entering Brazil: 2 litres of alcohol, 400 cigarettes (20 packs) and 25 cigars, gifts and other articles not exceeding a value of US$500.

Departing

From the centre of Rio, the international airport is about a 40-minute drive. Departure tax is included in flights at the time of purchase.

Electricity

Supplies are a mixture of 220V (e.g. Brasilia and Recife) and 127V (e.g. Rio and São Paulo). Countrywide a dual flat- or round-pin plug arrangement is used. Many of the newest hotels provide both outlets, but a world travel adaptor is essential.

Internet and email

Internet cafés can be found in all the main tourist areas. Off the beaten track, they are less plentiful. In business and luxury hotels, WiFi is increasingly available.

Money

Brazil's currency is the *real*; prices are marked 'R$' or often just '$'. Notes currently in circulation are R$100, 50, 10, 5, 2 and 1. Coins are in denominations of R$1, and 50, 25, 10, 5, and 1 *centavos*; there are 100 *centavos* to the *real*. Even a R$100 note can be difficult to change in some shops and bars, so try to keep hold of small notes.

ATMs are plentiful in cities and are found in most large beach resorts. Look for your card symbol on the machine as many accept only Brazilian bank cards. Carrying your debit or credit card is much safer than large amounts of cash, and is more convenient than traveller's cheques; these can be changed at certain hotels, or at the plentiful *cambios* and banks, but allow plenty of time for the transaction at the latter.

Opening hours

Banks are open from 10am to 4pm (Monday–Friday).

Museums usually follow normal office hours, but many close on Mondays.

Offices and businesses are generally open from 9am to 6pm (Monday–Friday), but close for lunch from around noon to 2pm.

Shops open from 10am and close at 7 or 8pm (Monday–Saturday). Large shopping centres usually stay open till 10pm or even midnight on some evenings and are open on Sundays too.

Passports and visas

Tourists from the United Kingdom, South Africa and New Zealand do not need a visa for holidays of less than 90 days, but residents of the US and Canada do, and must obtain one before they leave home. Anyone entering the country must have a passport valid for at least six months from the date of entry.

Pharmacies

Common medicines like antibiotics can be bought in a *farmácia* (chemist/drug store) quite cheaply and without restrictions. Pharmacists are generally quite helpful with regard to minor ailments. Some pharmacies in Rio, such as **City Farma** in Ipanema (*Rua Gomes Carneiro 144A. Tel: (21) 2247 3000*) are open 24 hours and deliver too.

Post

Mail is generally reliable, but postcards home will take at least two weeks. Look out for the blue and yellow CORREIOS (post office and post box) signs.

You can bypass post-office queues by asking your hotel to send postcards.

Ipanema Post Office. Rua Visconde de Pirajá 452. Tel: (21) 2563 8568.

Public holidays

1 January	Ano Novo (New Year's Day)
Saturday–Ash Wednesday	Carnaval (five days)
April/May precedes Páscoa	Good Friday, (Easter Sunday)
21 April	Tiradentes Day
1 May	Labour Day
62 days after Good Friday	Corpus Christi
7 September	Independence Day
12 October	Nossa Senhora de Aparecida (Brazil's patron saint)
2 November	All Souls' Day
15 November	Republic Day
25 December	Natal (Christmas)

In addition to the above, there are various regional pubic holidays, such as the Founding of Rio de Janeiro Day (20 January) and the Founding of São Paulo Day (25 January).

Suggested reading

Books

Blessed Anastacia: Women, Race and Christianity in Brazil by John Burdick (1998). A dazzling work that illustrates that the race issue in Brazil is still a current one.

Child of the Dark: The Diary of Carolina Maria de Jesus by Carolina Maria de Jesus (2003). A personal account of Brazilian *favela* life in the 1950s.
A Death in Brazil by Peter Robb (2003). An unusual mix of lucid, touching travelogue and incisive investigative journalism. A must-read.
Terra: Struggle of the Landless by Sebastião Salgado (1997). Outstanding photojournalism covering 16 years of the landless movement's struggle.

Websites

www.bahia-online.net A thoughtful guide to Bahia; the music section is particularly interesting.
www.brazilmax.com An excellent, insightful site with fascinating articles and great links.
www.infobrazil.com Brazilian current affairs, analysis and opinion.
www.ipanema.com An insider's guide to Rio.
www.maria-brazil.org Lively, personal, with a cookbook, music downloads and even Maria's little black book.
www.sonia-portuguese.com An introduction to Brazilian Portuguese.
www.terra-brazil.com Tour company site, but lots of intelligent information and inspirational, environmentally friendly tours.

Tax

A 5 per cent accommodation tax is added to hotel bills, but there is no retail or sales tax in Brazil.

Telephones

Area codes

Angra dos Reis, Ilha Grande, Paraty	24
Belém	91
Belo Horizonte (Ouro Preto)	31
Brasília	61
Búzios	22
Florianópolis	48
Fortaleza	85
Foz do Iguaçu	45
Manaus	92
Natal	84
Olinda, Recife, Fernando de Noronha	81
Rio de Janeiro	21
Salvador	71
São Paulo	11

To dial long distance within the country, you must prefix the above area codes with '0' and a two-digit 'service provider' code (for simplicity, stick with '21' which works in most places). So, if you are in Rio, calling a Manaus number listed as 3222 4312, dial 0-21-92-3222-4312.

To dial a Brazilian number from abroad, dial the international access code (usually 00) followed by '55' (Brazil's international dialling code), then the area code above, and finally the local number.

The cheapest way to make either a national or international phone call is from a payphone with a calling card bought in kiosks or newsagents; these have their own dialling rules.

Mobiles

Calls from your own mobile are expensive (a tri-band phone is needed with roaming activated). Even if your phone is unlocked, obtaining a local sim card can be difficult without Brazilian ID. Another option is to hire a mobile phone at the airport when you arrive, though call rates on these are high.

Time differences

The most visited parts of Brazil are notionally GMT minus three hours. This is true of Rio de Janeiro, São Paulo, Bahia and Minas Gerais. Brazilian summer time starts in October and ends in early February. During this period, Brazil's clocks go forward one hour in most of the southeast, just when most northern hemisphere countries are putting their clocks back one hour and coming off summer time. So, from March to October, when Brazil is on normal time and the UK is on its summer time, the time difference between Rio and London is four hours. This drops to just two hours when Brazil goes on to summer time and the UK comes off.

TIME ZONES

When it's noon in Rio, times in other countries are as follows:

	approx. Mar–Oct	approx. Oct–Feb
Auckland	3am (+1 day)	3am (+1 day)
Cape Town	5pm	4pm
London	4pm (BST)	2pm (GMT)
Los Angeles	8am (PDT)	6am (PST)
New York	11am (EDT)	9am (EST)
Sydney	1am (+1 day)	1am (+1 day)
Toronto	11am (EDT)	9am (EST)

Toilets

Don't flush paper in the bowl as the sanitary system (other than those in international hotels) can't cope with it; instead, put it in the bin provided. Note that the word for toilet is *banheiro* and bath is *banho*. Public loos are few and far between, but you should have no problem popping into a bar or restaurant to use their facilities.

Travellers with disabilities

Facilities for those with disabilities are woefully inadequate in many regions of the country. However, some new hotels around the country now provide at least one room suitable for visitors with a disability, and the waterfalls at Iguaçu, for example, have been wheelchair accessible for some time. **Access-able** (*www.access-able.com*) is a good source of information for travellers with disabilities.

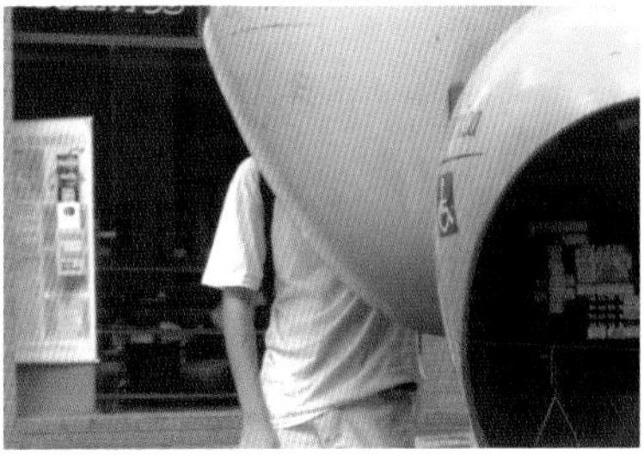

Buy a phonecard for cheap calls home

Language

Brazilians speak their own version of Portuguese, and while many of the word forms and letter accents may seem familiar to Spanish speakers, the sounds are truly unique. A number of websites offer introductions to Brazilian Portuguese and may be quite helpful; *www.sonia-portuguese.com* is a good starting point.

Vowels

Nasal vowels (crowned like *ã*, or followed by *n* or *m*) take some getting used to. *Não* (meaning 'no') is pronounced like 'noun', without the hard ending. In other instances, vowels are pronounced as follows:

a	'ah' or 'uh'
e	'e' as in 'egg'
i	'ee'
o	variously 'au' as in 'taught', 'o' as in 'or', and 'ou' as in 'you'
u	by itself 'ou', or 'w' when followed by another vowel

Consonants

Pronunciation of consonants is no less complicated and changes depending on the context. Some examples are:

ç	's'
q	'k' as in 'kiss'
r	a rolled 'r', but 'h' at the beginning of a word
rr	'h' as in 'how'
x	'sh' as in 'ship'

Basic words and phrases

General vocabulary

ENGLISH	BRAZILIAN PORTUGUESE
Yes	*sim* (seem)
No	*não* ('noun' without the final 'n')
Please	*por favor* (por faVOR)

ENGLISH	BRAZILIAN PORTUGUESE
Thank you (very much)	*(muito) obrigado* ((mWEeto) obrigAdo)
	obrigada if the speaker is a woman
You're welcome	*de nada* (de NAda)
Hello	*oi* (oi)
Everything okay?	*tudo bem?* (toodOh beng)
Everything's fine	*tudo bom* (toodOh bom)
	(both can be the question or the answer)
Goodbye	*tchau* (chow)
Good morning/day	*bom dia* (bon jeeha)
Good afternoon	*boa tarde* (boh TARge)
Good evening/night	*boa noite* (boa noitchay)
Excuse me	*com licença* (com leeSENssa)
I'm sorry	*desculpe* (descoolPAY)
Help!	*socorro*! (soKoho)
Today	*hoje* (oijay)
Tomorrow	*amanhã* (amaNja)
Yesterday	*ontem* (onteNg)
Where?	*onde*? (onjay)
When?	*quando*? (KWANdo)
Why?	*por quê*? (poorKAY)
How?	*como*? (COmo)

Useful words and phrases

ENGLISH	BRAZILIAN PORTUGUESE
How much is it?	*quanto é*? (KWANtoe eh)
(Too) expensive	*(muito) caro* ((mWEeto) kARo)
I don't understand	*eu não entendo* (ehoo nah-oo entendo)
Do you speak English?	*você fala inglês?* (VohSay fallah eenGLEss)
My name is...	*meu nome é...* (mehoo noMAY eh...)

Emergencies

Emergency numbers

Ambulance *192*
Fire Department *193*
Civil Police *147*
Municipal Police *153*
Military Police *190*

Health

Insurance

Adequate health insurance is essential. There are good-value deals on the internet, but carefully check what is covered, particularly if you are planning adventure activities or travel to remote parts of Brazil. Annual cover costs little more than single-trip policies and is well worth investigating.

Risks

In the Pantanal, dengue fever is a serious problem, and malaria is a risk in some parts of the country. There have been some cases of cholera in the northeast, and yellow fever occurs in large areas of north and west Brazil. It is advisable to consult your doctor at least two months before departure to verify all vaccination requirements.

Tap water in Brazil is heavily treated and you are advised to stick to bottled mineral water.

Safety and crime

Most visitors experience no problems, but it pays to take precautions. Always ensure you have comprehensive travel insurance, and take copies of all travel documents. Keep a note of your credit card replacement phone numbers.

Drugs

Drugs are a big problem in Brazil, and penalties for possession are stiff – even for small amounts of marijuana. Police target tourists for drug searches, in the hope of extorting bribes.

Money scams

Don't accept offers to change money on street corners; fake notes abound. Always check your change, and if you are handing over a large note, make sure the denomination is clearly seen.

Muggings and theft

Never resist an attacker who demands your valuables; many will resort to violence if challenged. Consider spreading your cash and cards between different pockets, so that, if pickpocketed, you don't lose everything. Only carry as much as you need, stay alert and avoid unlit or unpopulated areas, especially at night. Do not openly display cash or expensive cameras and jewellery.

Reporting petty crime can be time-consuming, and the police will often discourage you. For insurance purposes, a better option may be to file an internet report; this is possible in the states of Rio (*www.delegaciavirtual.rj.gov.br*) and São Paulo (*www.policiacivil.sp.gov.br*). Ask a local's help if you don't understand Portuguese.

Embassies and consulates

If you get into trouble with the police, have an accident, lose your passport, or become a victim of crime, you might need to contact your embassy or consulate. If you're planning a lengthy stay it's also a good idea to register with them. Most countries have their embassies in Brasilia. The addresses of the consular offices in Rio (or São Paulo) are given here, together with websites linking to other consular offices and embassies. Always check your government's advice before you travel.

Australia

Australian Consulate. *Veirano and Associates, Avenida Presidente Wilson 231, 23rd floor, Rio. Tel: (21) 3824 4624. www.brazil.embassy.gov.au*

Canada

Canadian Consulate General. *Avenida Atlântica 1130, 5th floor, Atlântica Business Center, Copacabana, Rio. Tel: (21) 2543 3004. www.dfait-maeci.gc.ca*

New Zealand

New Zealand Consulate-General. *Alameda Campinas 579, 15th floor, São Paulo. Tel: (11) 3148 0616. www.nzembassy.com*

South Africa

South African Honorary Consulate. *Rua David Campista 50, Rio. Tel: (21) 2527 1455. www.dfa.gov.za/foreign*

UK

British Consulate-General. *Praia do Flamengo 284, 2nd floor, Rio. Tel: (21) 2555 9600. www.britishembassy.gov.uk*

US

US Consulate. *Avenida Presidente Wilson 147, Rio. Tel: (21) 2292 7117. http://brasilia.usembassy.gov*

Being a police officer is not always a chore

Directory

Accommodation price guide

A scale of one to four stars has been used as a price guide, with one star indicating the cheapest option and four stars the most expensive. Price bands are based on the average cost of a double room in local currency. Often an additional bed can be added to a room for a fraction of the total. Credit cards are widely accepted in the cities, but not always in remote villages or beachside *pousadas*. If you are planning to pay with a card, check it is accepted at the time of booking. (Note that some of the websites listed in this section will not work on Apple Mac systems equipped with the Safari browser. If you encounter problems, try using Internet Explorer on a PC.)

★	under R$100
★★	R$100 to R$200
★★★	R$200 to R$300
★★★★	Over R$300

Eating out price guide

The star system is based on the average price of a meal for one person without drinks or tips.

★	under R$20
★★	R$20 to R$40
★★★	R$40 to R$80
★★★★	Over R$80

Rio de Janeiro

Accommodation

Rio Hostel Ipanema ★
Simple dormitory accommodation and one double room; all with shared bathroom, and just three blocks from the beach.
Rua Barão da Torre 175, Casa 14, Ipanema, Rio. Tel: (21) 2247 7269. www.justfly.com.br

Casa Mango Mango ★–★★
A range of rooms from dormitory to en suite in a bargain-priced historic house with tropical gardens.
Rua Joaquim Murtinho 587, Santa Teresa, Rio. Tel: (21) 2508 6440. www.casamangomango.com

Izzy Rent ★★–★★★
Apartments in Copacabana and Ipanema. Efficient, English-speaking service, but make sure that the price includes cleaning and any extras.
Rua Djalma Ulrich 163, Copacabana, Rio. Tel: (21) 2522 7810. www.ttabrazil.com

Arpoador Inn ★★★
On a spectacular beach location, although rooms and service are often lacking. Pay more for a seafront room and go to

sleep to the sound of surf, rather than traffic.
Rua Francisco Otaviano 177, Ipanema, Rio. Tel: (21) 2523 0060.

Galápagos Inn ★★★
A member of the prestigious Roteiros de Charme group *(see 'Accommodation', p137)* in a central location with verandas looking out to João Fernandinho beach, where the hotel offers bar service.
Praia João Fernandinho 3, Búzios. Tel: (22) 2623 2245. www.galapagos.com.br

Solar de Santa ★★★
A laid-back colonial guesthouse in the vibrant centre of this artistic enclave. With tasteful rooms, helpful, attentive staff and a cool terrace in hillside gardens, this place is a real find.
Ladeira do Meireles 32, Santa Teresa, Rio. Tel: (21) 2221 2117. www.solardesanta.com

La Maison ★★★★
An exquisite 'house' straight out of a design magazine, with personal service and a pool with views of Christ the Redeemer.
58 Rua Sérgio Porto, Gávea, Rio. Tel: (21) 3205 3585. www.lamaisonario.com

Eating out

Chez Michou ★
There are plenty of swanky places to eat in Búzios, but this crêperie is quick, good and inexpensive – where locals and visitors alike congregate.
Av. José Bento Ribeiro Dantas 90, Búzios. Tel: (22) 2623 2169.

New Natural Restaurant ★–★★
A *comida a quilo* (food by weight) restaurant. Great location, perfect for buying a healthy takeaway lunch to eat on the beach. (Look out for the *comida a quilo* sign everywhere in Rio for cheap (fairly decent) food to eat in or take away.)
Rua Barão da Torre 173, Ipanema. Tel: (21) 2287 0301.

Aprazivel ★★★
High up in the hills of Santa Teresa with wonderful views. It has its own fully stocked *cachaça* bar and a tropical garden restaurant serving imaginative Brazilian food.
Rua Aprazível 62, Santa Teresa, Rio. Tel: (21) 3852 4935. www.aprazivel.com.br

Espirito Santa ★★★
Exotic fruit, nuts and fish dishes from the Amazon, spicy seafood stews from Salvador, and cowboy beef dishes from down south. A relaxing outdoor balcony and wonderful service too.
Rua Almirante Alexandrino 264, Santa Teresa, Rio. Tel: (21) 2508 7095. www.espiritosanta.com.br

Sushi Leblon ★★★
You have to book, and fellow diners can be pretentious, but this is probably the best sushi in Rio, and service is faultless.
Rua Dias Ferreira 256, Leblon, Rio. Tel: (21) 2512 7830.

Porcão ★★★★
This chain of all-you-can-eat *rodízio churrascarias (see 'Entertainment', p143)* with salad and sushi bar is a real experience.

Arrive hungry and don't be rushed. There are several locations, but this one has views of Sugarloaf and is fabulous at sunset.
Avenida Infante Dom Henrique, Parque do Flamengo, Rio.
Tel: (21) 2554 8535.

Entertainment

Academia da Cachaça
A small bar crammed with 500 bottles of *cachaça*; take your time. *Feijoada* is served weekdays until 4pm.
Rua Conde de Bernadotte 26, Leblon, Rio. Tel: (21) 2529 2680.
www.academiadacachaca.com.br

Bar Semente
Live samba, salsa and cheap cocktails next to Lapa's famous arches.
Rua Joaquim Silva 138, Lapa, Rio.
Tel: (21) 2242 5165.

Bunker 94
Close to Ipanema, three rooms of sound and two dance floors, with a friendly crowd. Everything from classic soul and '80s music to drum and bass depending on the night and the room.
Rua Raul Pompeia 94, Copacabana, Rio. Tel: (21) 2521 0367.

Casarão Cultural dos Arcos
Live music nights mixing up Brazilian and Cuban sounds. Fine DJs and lots of happy souls.
Avenida Mem de Sá 23, Lapa, Rio.
Tel: (21) 2266 1014.
www.loud.com.br/casarao

Copacabana Palace
This grand old institution attracts rich businessmen, but the poolside bar is a nice place to kick off the evening with a cocktail.
Avenida Atlântica 1702, Copacabana, Rio de Janeiro.
Tel: (21) 2548 7070.
www.copacabanapalace.com.br

Devassa
Rio's first microbrewery is now in several locations in the city. Expect tourists and drinkers out to impress.
Rua General San Martin 1241, Leblon, Rio. Tel: (21) 2540 6087.

Nova Lounge
Big promoters host a wide variety of nights, from bossa nova to house.
Rua Barão da Torre 334, Ipanema, Rio. Tel: (21) 3813 1663.

Rio Scenarium
Can be touristy at times, but this three-storey warehouse is still one of Rio's best bars. Regular live music.
Rua do Lavradio 20, Lapa, Rio.
Tel: (21) 3147 9005.
www.rioscenarium.com.br

00 (Zero Zero)
Part of the dome in Gavea's planetarium, this is a beautiful bar, restaurant and club with people to match.
Rua Padre Leonel Franca 240, Gavea, Rio.
Tel: (21) 2540 8041.

Sports and leisure

Bike&Lazer
When they close the beach road on Sundays, a bicycle is a great way to sample Rio's beach scene. Bike&Lazer are close to the beach and rent reliable machines.
Rua Visconde de Pirajá

135B, Ipanema, Rio. Tel: (21) 2521 2686.

Just Fly

Paulo Celani is the calm operator of this established, professional outfit, offering the chance to hang-glide from the top of the Tijuaca forest down onto the beach. They offer forest jeep tours too.
Tel: (21) 2268 0565 or (21) 9985 7540. www.justfly.com.br

Luiz Marcos Football

If you want to see a game with a local guide in Rio or elsewhere in Brazil without the premiums charged by the big operators, contact Luiz.
www.ofutebol.com (for fixture lists), luiz@futebolthebrazilianwayoflife.com (for tickets)

Rio Hiking

An established all-rounder offering diving, rock climbing and other adventure sports, as well as treks though the Tijuaca forest, day trips to Petrópolis and outings deep into the Atlantic forest. Nightlife tours of Rio too.
Tel: (21) 2552 9204 or (21) 9721 0594. www.riohiking.com.br

Terra Brazil

Fascinating trips off the beaten track that give a real insight into the country, while respecting the environment and local people. Tours throughout Brazil too.
Rua da Passagem 83, Sala 314, Botafogo, Rio de Janeiro. Tel: (21) 2543 3185. www.terra-brazil.com

Costa Verde

Accommodation

Go native ★–★★★★

Resort hotels on quieter parts of Ilha Grande have a reputation for mediocre food and overpriced transport, while *pousadas* in the main town tend to be quite basic. Rent a house from a local instead; anything from a simple cottage to a villa with all the facilities.
www.ilhagrande.com.br or www.aluguetemporada.com.br

Pousada do Corsário ★★

Comfortable rooms facing the mountains, each with a hammock outside. Tranquil, riverside location just a five-minute walk from the historic centre.
Rua João do Prado 26, Chácara, Paraty. Tel: (24) 3371 1866. www.pousadadocorsario.com.br

Pousada Guapuruvu ★★

A short walk from the centre of the village, this is a basic little place in the forest. A thatched breakfast area overlooks a stream, and the owners will recommend a friend's place if they are full.
Rua do Bicão 299, Vila do Abraão, Ilha Grande. Tel: (24) 3361 5081 or (21) 9949 3627. www.imagelink.com.br/users/mpdabreu

Pestana Angra ★★★

Intimate resort hotel with private beach and spa, though rather isolated. All bungalows have sea views; some also have Jacuzzis.
Estrada Vereador Benedito Adelino 3700, Retiro, Angra dos Reis. Tel: (24) 3364 2005. www.pestana.com

Pousada do Sandi ★★★

In the historic centre of Paraty, friendly and

family-run. Good restaurant, pool and sauna. The best rooms have a balcony overlooking the quiet cobbled street.
Largo do Rosário 1, Paraty. Tel: (11) 3864 9111 (weekdays), (24) 3371 1236 (weekends). www.pousadadosandi.com.br

Eating out

Corsário Negro ★★
One of the best seafood diners on Ilha Grande. Fresh lobster and the paella are highlights.
Rua Alice Kury 90, Vila do Abraão, Ilha Grande. Tel: (24) 3361 5321.

Punto Di Vino ★★★★
Superb, authentic Italian food; wood-fired pizza, fish ravioli and sublime chocolate mousse, all served in a convivial atmosphere with live music in the internal courtyard. The locals' favourite.
Rua Marechal Deodoro da Fonseca 129, Paraty. Tel: (24) 3371 1348.

Entertainment

Bar do Dinho
Late in the evening, this rustic but fun place is filled with locals and a few tourists, all there for the live music and lively dancing.
Rua da Matriz, Paraty. Tel: (24) 3371 1790.

Beach bars
Too plentiful to mention individually, they are dotted all over the Costa Verde, some on tiny uninhabited islands. Ask a local for a recommendation, or organise a leisurely 'boat crawl' with Angatu (*see below*).

Café Paraty
Always busy, this is a touristy restaurant and bar but with good music most nights.
Rua do Comércio 253, Paraty. Tel: (24) 3371 0128.

Sport and leisure

Angatu
Outstanding, tailor-made trips, mostly by boat, around Paraty, Ilha Grande and Angra dos Reis. This company shows real concern for the environment and will meet all your needs; they also rent villas.
Avenida Pacaembú 1702, São Paulo. Tel: (11) 3872 0945. www.angatu.com

Paraty Adventure
Unlike some agencies who think ecotourism refers to any outdoor activity, this company really is 'green'. It offers a range of boat trips, beach tours and the gold trail, as well as some special visits to traditional communities.
Praça do Chafariz. Tel: (24) 3371 6135. www.paratyadventure.com

Terra Brazil
Fascinating trips off the beaten track that give a real insight into the country, while respecting the environment and local people. Tours throughout Brazil too.
Rua da Passagem 83, Sala 314, Botafogo, Rio de Janeiro. Tel: (21) 2543 3185. www.terra-brazil.com

The south

Accommodation

Bourbon ★★
In the centre of São

Paulo, close to the Theatro Municipal. Chain hotel but with individual touches that make all the difference.
Avenida Vieira de Carvalho 99, Centro, São Paulo.
Tel: (11) 3337 1414.
www.bourbon.com.br

Pousada Penareia ★★
Relaxing 13-room getaway on the island of Santa Catarina, looking out to the sea. Room décor is pleasing and breakfasts are plentiful.
Praia da Armãçao, Ilha Santa Catarina.
Tel: (48) 3338 1616.
www.pousadapenareia.com.br

Pousada da Vigia ★★★
Small luxury hotel on the northernmost point of the island. Great views over the beach and a full range of facilities.
Rua Cônego Walmor Castro 291, Praia Lagoinha, Ilha Santa Catarina.
Tel: (48) 3284 1789.
www.pousadadavigia.com.br

Emiliano ★★★
Spacious luxury, a rooftop spa with marble plunge pool, and flawless service without fuss make this a splurge worth remembering. In the Jardims district which is full of upmarket designer boutiques.
Rua Oscar Freire 384, Jardims, São Paulo.
Tel: (11) 3069 4369.
www.emiliano.com.br

Tropical das Cataratas ★★★★
Pricey, luxurious hotel perched on the edge of the famous falls.
Rodovia BR-469 km28, Parque Nacional do Iguaçu.
Tel: (45) 3521 7000.
www.tropicalhotel.com.br

Eating out

Bar do Arante ★
On the south coast, this island institution serves outstanding seafood and fish. Notes scribbled on napkins by travellers have been kept for posterity and festoon the walls and ceiling.
Rua Abelardo Gomes 254, Praia do Pântano do Sul, Ilha Santa Catarina. Tel: (48) 3237 7022.

Bráz ★★
Perfect pizza and old-school service with a hustle and bustle that is noisy but doesn't grate. Check the website for other branches.
Rua Vupabussu 271, Pinheiros, São Paulo.
Tel: (11) 3037 7975.
www.casabraz.com.br

Villa Magionne ★★
An intimate, romantic spot overlooking the lake, serving Mediterranean food with a Brazilian twist.
Rua da Amizade 273, Lagoa da Conceição, Ilha Santa Catarina.
Tel: (48) 2232 6859.

Antiquarius ★★★
Excellent dishes of Portuguese origin in an elegant setting dotted with antiques and Brazilian art.
Alameda Lorena 1884, Jardims, São Paulo.
Tel: (11) 3082 3015 or 3084 8686.

Entertainment

El Divino
Armchairs and sofas on the beach, and uplifting house and hip hop, all in this hugely entertaining club. There's a spacious indoor lounge bar and a

restaurant as well.
Avenida dos Pampos (and other locations), Jurerê Internacional, Ilha Santa Catarina.
Tel: (48) 3282 1816.
www.eldivinobrasil.com.br

Latitude 27°
Live music and wild dancing into the early hours. Close to the lake, this is a great spot to end up after an evening of bar hopping.
Rodovia Jornalista Manuel de Menezes 565, Lagoa da Conceição, Ilha Santa Catarina.
Tel: (48) 3232 5841.
www.latitude27.com.br

Rey Castro
After 11pm this bar and restaurant transforms into a nightclub, with all-night Latin rhythms. Free salsa classes on Wednesdays.
Jesuino Cardoso 181, Vila Olimpia, São Paulo. Tel: (11) 3044 4383.
www.reycastro.com.br

Skye Bar
Perched on top of the Hotel Unique. Join the beautiful people for sunset cocktails by the pool.
Avenida Brigadeiro Luís Antônio 4700, Jardims, São Paulo.
Tel: (11) 3055 4700.

Sports and leisure

Adrena Ilha
Surf and sea-kayak lessons, rock climbing, mountain bike and hiking tours are just some of the activities available.
Rua das Gaivotas 610, Praia dos Ingleses, Ilha Santa Catarina.
Tel: (48) 3269 1414.
www.adrenailha.com.br

The centre

Accommodation

Note that for the Pantanal, accommodation pricing reflects the fact that all meals and tours are included.

Hotel Tijuco ★★
An elegant Niemeyer creation from the 1950s which still contains the original furniture. The more expensive rooms have balconies.
Rua Macau do Meio 211, Diamantina.
Tel: (38) 3531 1022.

Pousada Pé da Serra ★★
Friendly, family-run guesthouse with an outdoor pool set in tranquil green gardens. Good central location and filling breakfasts.
Rua Nicolau Panzera 51, Tiradentes.
Tel: (32) 3355 1107.
www.pedaserra.com.br

Grande Hotel de Ouro Preto ★★★
Designed by Niemeyer in the 1940s, this is a modernist hotel but sympathetic to the surrounding colonial architecture. Room balconies (and the veranda of Perypatus, the hotel restaurant) have great views of the town.
Rua das Flores 164, Ouro Preto.
Tel: (31) 3551 1488.
www.hotelouropreto.com.br

Pousada do Mondego ★★★
Occupying an 18th-century mansion next to the Igreja de São Francisco, each of the 22 rooms is tastefully furnished and spacious.
Largo de Coimbra 38, Ouro Preto. Tel: (31) 3551 2040.
www.mondego.com.br

Xaraés ★★★
Part of a working cattle

ranch next to a river in the Pantanal. It has a pool, sauna and all facilities but was built and is run with full consideration of the environment. Full range of tours offered.
Fazenda Xaraés, Estrada Parque km17, Abobral, Corumbá, Pantanal.
Tel: (67) 9906 9272.
www.xaraes.com.br

Refúgio Ecológico Caiman ★★★★
A true pioneer of ecological tourism, this award-winning Pantanal eco-lodge is also a centre for scientific research and the Arara Azul (Blue Macaw) Project. Expect rustic accommodation and a variety of tours, including the chance to take part in a cattle drive.
For reservations: Avenida Brigadeiro Faria Lima 3015, suite 161, São Paulo.
Tel: (11) 3706 1800.
www.caiman.com.br

Eating out

Chafariz do Paço ★★
Dona Teresa has been laying out the buffet here for 25 years. Open for lunch only, but worth a visit for her local cuisine and the family heirlooms that decorate the walls.
Rua São José 167, Ouro Preto. Tel: (31) 3551 2828

Le Coq d'Or ★★
One of Brazil's best restaurants, mixing French Cordon Bleu with Brazilian cuisine. Part of the Solar Nossa Senhora do Rosario hotel, which was built in 1830 and has just undergone extensive renovation.
Rua Getúlio Vargas 270, Ouro Preto.
Tel: (31) 3551 5200.
www.hotelsolardorosario.com.br

Padre Toledo ★★
It doesn't look much, but housed in an 18th-century house, right in the historic centre of the town, it offers Minas regional cuisine at its best. Basic but functional rooms are also available in the attached *pousada*.
Rua Direita 250, Tiradentes.
Tel: (32) 3355 2132.
www.padretoledo.com.br

Entertainment

Bar do Beco
Cachaça cocktails are the speciality in this early-opening, late-closing bar. Live music some nights.
Travessa do Arieira 15, Ouro Preto. Tel: (031) 3551 1429.

Sports and leisure

Caminho Real Turismo
Organises hiking tours along the Estrada Real, or less strenuous minibus trips to the colonial towns along the historic gold trail.
Rua Benjamim Machado 340, Ouro Preto.
Tel: (31) 3551 1078 or (31) 9961 1818.
www.ouropreto.com.br/caminhorealtur

Bahia

Accommodation

Hotel Canto das Águas ★★
Deserved member of the Roteiros de Charme group as well as being environmentally friendly. Beautiful hotel on the river, with a pool too.
Avenida Senhor dos Passos 1, Lençóis, Chapada Diamantina.
Tel: (75) 3334 1154.
www.lencois.com.br

Pousada Farol das Tartarugas ★★
Peaceful beachfront location on the edge of town. Intimate and rustic with four cottages, it's a more modest version of the large eco-resort. There's a swimming pool and garden with hammocks as well.
Rua Martim Pescador, Quadra 61, Praia do Forte. Tel: (71) 3676 1515. www.faroldastartarugas.com.br

Pousada Red Fish ★★★
Simple yet very stylish, owned by a charming English artist. Excellent breakfast and service; highly recommended.
Ladeira do Boqueirão 1, Salvador.
Tel: (71) 3243 8473.
www.hotelredfish.com.br

Convento do Carmo ★★★★
Elegant, converted 16th-century monastery combining history with 5-star luxury. Undoubtedly the best place to stay in Salvador.
Rua do Carmo 1, Salvador. Tel: (71) 3327 8400. www.pestana.com

Estrela d'Água ★★★★
Exquisitely designed *pousada* on the beach, with a pool. A member of Roteiros de Charme, with a Relais & Chateaux restaurant. High prices but high quality and very romantic.
Estrada Arraial d'Ajuda, Trancoso.
Tel: (73) 3668 1030.
www.estreladagua.com.br

Eating out

Bahianas ★
You can't go to Bahia and not sample the delights of these women street-sellers dressed in white. The food is fried so is pretty safe. Try *acaraje*, a spicy prawn pattie.

Axego ★★
Food made with love; huge portions and a long-time favourite. Try *moqueca de camarão*, a Bahian prawn curry, or make your visit an occasion for *feijoada* on Sunday.
Rua João de Deus 1 (upstairs), Salvador.
Tel: (71) 3242 7481.

GOA ★★★
Nightly candle-lit, all-you-can-eat Brazilian buffet from 7.30pm served inside a Polynesian-style thatched building or on the lawn next to the sea.
Avenida do Farol, Praia do Forte.
Tel: (71) 3676 4000.
www.brasilecoresortspa.com

Estrela d'Água ★★★★
One of the best restaurants in the whole region. Enjoy world-class cuisine on the terrace or in the garden.
Estrada Arraial d'Ajuda, Trancoso.
Tel: (73) 3668 1030.
www.estreladagua.com.br

Entertainment

Balé Folclórico da Bahia
Wonderful performances of dance and capoeira. Check the website for the latest details and times.
Teatro Miguel Santana, Rua Gregório de Matos 49, Pelourinho, Salvador.
Tel: (71) 3322 1962.
http://balefolcloricodabahia.com.br

Tourist information

The helpful staff of the tourist office in Salvador can provide you with a free copy of

Day and Night, which details all performances for that week and can provide city guides for a fee. **Disque Turismo** up the road (*No 131*) offers English-speaking assistance.
12 Rua das Laranjeiras. Tel: (71) 3321 2463. www.emtursa.ba.gov.br

Sport and leisure

Centro Tour
Bike and horse riding trips, canoeing and hiking, as well as whale and night-time turtle watching.
Avenida ACM, Praia do Forte. Tel: (71) 3676 1091. www.centroturistico.com.br

Praia do Forte Eco Resort
Offers full activities and tours to their guests.
Avenida do Farol, Praia do Forte. Tel: (71) 3676 4000. www.brasilecoresortspa.com

Costa do Sauípe Resort
Tel: (71) 0800 702 0203. www.costadosauipe.com.br

Terra Brazil
Excellent, insightful city tours and *candomblé* shows in Salvador, sailing trips to Itaparica, day trips to Praia do Forte and walking and four-wheel-drive tours in Chapada Diamantina (*see 'Getting away from it all', pp126–7*).
Rua da Passagem 83, Sala 314, Botafogo, Rio de Janeiro. Tel: (21) 2543 3185. www.terra-brazil.com

The northeast

Accommodation

Pousada Vila Kalango ★★
Suitably rustic and made with local materials, unlike some of the newer offerings in Jericoacoara. Lovely lounge with hammocks overlooking the dunes and beach, and romantic cabins on stilts.
Rua das Dunas 30, Jericoacoara. Tel: (88) 3669 2289. www.vilakalango.com.br

Pousada do Amparo ★★★
Wonderful views from this 18th-century building with furniture to match, plus three terraces, a pool and a restaurant with a garden.
Rua do Amparo 191, Olinda. Tel: (81) 3439 1749. www.pousadadoamparo.com.br

Toca da Coruja Pousada ★★★
Gorgeous. A member of the Roteiros de Charme group. Tropical garden and fusion restaurant. Romantic and environmentally responsible.
Avenida Baia dos Golfinhos, Pipa. Tel: (84) 3246 2226. www.tocadacoruja.com.br (Portuguese only).

Pousada Maravilha ★★★★
One of the few luxury places to stay on the island. Stylish, Balinese-inspired, private bungalows built to integrate with the environment, and a beautiful pool area.
Rodovia BR-363, Sueste, Parque Nacional Fernando de Noronha. Tel: (81) 3619 0162. www.pousadamaravilha.com.br

Eating out

Chica Pitanga ★
This 'food by weight' restaurant is not only a

bargain but a great way to sample local dishes. Enjoy a full range of salads, meat, fish and pasta dishes as well as desserts.
Rua Petrolina 19, Boa Viagem beach, Recife. Tel: (81) 3465 2224. www.chicapitanga.com.br

Mangai ★★
A charming place that prides itself on its ethics as well as its food. Excellent regional food served buffet-style, perfect for sampling lots of dishes. Very good value.
Avenida Amintas Barros 3300, Lagoa Nova, Natal. Tel: (84) 3206 3344. www.mangai.com.br

Oficina do Sabor ★★★
Regional cuisine with a modern twist and one of the best restaurants around. Long established and very popular, so try to book; the lovely veranda is the nicest place to sit.
Rua do Amparo 335, Olinda. Tel: (81) 3429 3331. www.oficinadosabor.com

Entertainment

Alto da Sé
This square in Olinda is the best spot for a drink and some street food at weekends, particularly Sunday, when it fills up with locals for an impromptu party.

Bar do Pirata
An enormous club that is very commercial but fun and welcomes people of all ages and persuasions. Monday is the big night. Seven hours of live, mostly *forró*, music starts early for Brazil – at 8pm.
Rua dos Tabajaras 325, Fortaleza. Tel: (85) 4011 6161. www.pirata.com.br

Pátio de São Pedro
This historic square in Recife hosts cultural events and live music and is a lively spot most evenings, with people spilling out of the many surrounding bars and restaurants.
www.patiodesaopedro.ceci-br.org

Sport and leisure

Catamaran Tours
Boat trips along the rivers, around the bay and to islands around Recife.
Cais das Cinco Pontas, Recife. Tel: (81) 3424 2845. www.catamarantours.com.br

Dune buggy rides
There are plenty of *bugreiros* (buggy riders) touting for work up and down the coast wherever there are dunes nearby, but make sure they are licensed and respectful of the environment.
Rua Guilherme Tinoco 1274, Bairro do Tirol, Natal. Tel: (84) 9982 3162. www.buggyecia.com.br

The Amazon

A selection of Amazon jungle lodges has been covered in the 'Destination guide' section of this book (*see 'Into the jungle', p118*). The lodges provide accommodation and all meals, as well as guided tours into the jungle and along the river.

Accommodation

Equatorial Palace ★★
Near the Museu Paraense Emílio Goeldi (*see*

Belém, p114), the Palace has 126 rooms (with air con) which are being upgraded in stages. Ask for one that has been renovated.
Avenida Braz de Aguiar 602, Nazaré, Belém. Tel: (91) 3241 2000.

Mango Guest House ★★
Delightful 'jungle' guesthouse in Manaus, with links to upriver eco-lodges. It's much better than many of the large city hotels, but the out-of-the-centre location isn't good for those who want to explore the city.
Rua Flavio Espirito Santo 1, Kissia II, Manaus. Tel: (92) 3656 6033. www.naturesafaris.com.br

Ana Cássia Palace Hotel ★★★
It's a tower hotel but in a good location close to the floating docks. Fine views from the restaurant and rooftop pool. Rooms have air con.
Rua dos Andradas 14, Centro, Manaus. Tel: (92) 3622 3637. hacassia@internext.com.br

Eating out / Entertainment

Amazon Beer ★
Tourist hangout that gets busy in the early evening. Good *feijoada* and Amazon shrimp, and the brewery produces its own beer.
Boulevard Castilho França, Estação das Docas, Galpão 1, Campina, Belém. Tel: (91) 3212 5400.

Açai e Cia ★★
Tasty Amazonian dishes, particularly the fish soups. Live music at the weekends.
Rua Acre 98, Flores, Manaus. Tel: (92) 3635 3637.

Index

Acknowledgements

The authors would like to thank: Franklin and family in Vidigal; all the students at Barbara Olivi's school in Rocinha; Julian Kenny; all at Hotel Solar de Santa in Rio; Terra Brazil; Angartu in Paraty.

Thomas Cook wishes to thank the photographers JANE EGGINTON and IAIN MACINTYRE, for the loan of the photographs reproduced in this book, to whom copyright in the photographs belongs (except the following):

WORLD PICTURES/PHOTOSHOT 1
TERRA BRAZIL 9, 36, 74, 76, 77, 98, 125, 135, 150
PARATY ADVENTURE 24, 153
EMBRATUR 5, 21, 23, 25, 81, 82, 84, 85, 86, 87, 97, 99, 109, 111, 124, 146, 151
AGÊNCIA BRASIL 107
EURICO ZIMBRES 15, 88
TITO VIANA MARTINS FILHO 60
WIKIMEDIA COMMONS 102 (Patrick-br), 103 (Sortica), 143 (LeRoc)
NASA 113
ROBERTO TIETZMANN 136
FERNANDO REBÊLO 141

Copy-editing: ANNE McGREGOR for CAMBRIDGE PUBLISHING MANAGEMENT LTD

Index: KAROLIN THOMAS for CAMBRIDGE PUBLISHING MANAGEMENT LTD

Maps: PCGRAPHICS, Old Woking, UK

Proofreading: JAN McCANN for CAMBRIDGE PUBLISHING MANAGEMENT LTD

SEND YOUR THOUGHTS TO
BOOKS@THOMASCOOK.COM

We're committed to providing the very best up-to-date information in our travel guides and constantly strive to make them as useful as they can be. You can help us to improve future editions by letting us have your feedback. If you've made a wonderful discovery on your travels that we don't already feature, if you'd like to inform us about recent changes to anything that we do include, or if you simply want to let us know your thoughts about this guidebook and how we can make it even better – we'd love to hear from you.

Send us ideas, discoveries and recommendations today and then look out for your valuable input in the next edition of this title.

Emails to the above address, or letters to Travellers Project Editor, Thomas Cook Publishing, PO Box 227, Coningsby Road, Peterborough PE3 8SB, UK.

Please don't forget to let us know which title your feedback refers to!